Awesome projects—in less than an hour!

DIY
T-SHIRT
CRAFTS

From Braided Bracelets
to Floor Pillows, **50** Unexpected
Ways to Recycle Your Old T-Shirts

— ADRIANNE SURIAN —

adamsmedia

Avon, Massachusetts

Published by
Adams Media, a division of F+W Media, Inc.
57 Littlefield Street, Avon, MA 02322. U.S.A.
www.adamsmedia.com

ISBN 10: 1-4405-8967-4
ISBN 13: 978-1-4405-8967-6
eISBN 10: 1-4405-8968-2
eISBN 13: 978-1-4405-8968-3

Printed in the United States of America.

10 9 8 7 6 5 4 3 2 1

Library of Congress Cataloging-in-Publication Data

Surian, Adrianne.
  DIY T-shirt crafts / Adrianne Surian.
     pages cm
  Includes index.
  ISBN 978-1-4405-8967-6 (pb) -- ISBN 1-4405-8967-4 (pb) -- ISBN 978-1-4405-8968-3 (ebook) -- ISBN 1-4405-8968-2 (ebook)
  1. T-shirts. I. Title.
  TT675.S87 2015
  687--dc23
                                    2015007096

Cover design by Sylvia McArdle.
Cover images by Adrianne Surian and © Sarawuth Pamoon/123RF.
Photos by Adrianne Surian.

This book is available at quantity discounts for bulk purchases.
For information, please call 1-800-289-0963.

C O N T

E N T S

INTRODUCTION

T-shirts. You wear them in, you wear them out. You lounge in them, work in them, and pick them up as souvenirs. A great T-shirt is a comfort, a wardrobe staple, and it's what you wear when making some of your best memories!

T-shirts don't last forever, though—you spill on them, stain them, and outgrow them. But now you don't have to agonize over sending them to the T-shirt graveyard. *DIY T-Shirt Crafts* gives you fifty innovative and useful ways to turn your old T-shirts into jewelry, accessories, home décor, and more! And you don't have to be an expert crafter to turn your T-shirts into works of art, either. Each project is designed with the beginning crafter in mind, works up quickly in an hour or less, and does not require the use of a sewing machine. In fact, some projects require little more than scissors and glue, and there are ways to use every part of a shirt here, right down to the scraps.

So whether you want to show off your style with a Braided Chain Statement Necklace or Rhinestone Button Boot Cuffs, update your home décor with a Braided Yarn Bowl or Bleached T-Shirt Canvas Art, or impress your friends with a Wine Bag, Decorated Mason Jar, or Baby Pompom Hat, *DIY T-Shirt Crafts* is here to help you give your old T-shirts new life. Enjoy!

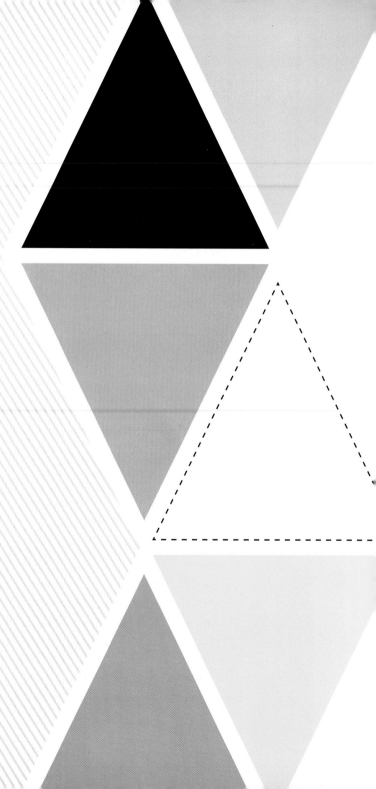

HOW TO MAKE T-SHIRT YARN

possible. Women's shirts usually have seams along the sides, because they are fitted, but men's shirts—the more basic, the better—are great for turning into yarn. The average men's XL shirt, cut 1" wide, will yield between 50 and 60 yards of T-Shirt Yarn, which is comparable to buying a skein of boutique yarn, and is enough to make one (or several) of the projects you will find here. To easily turn a T-shirt into a skein of yarn, just grab your T-shirt and a pair of scissors, and follow these steps.

1. First, cut the body panel off the shirt just below the arms, and remove the bottom hem. Do save these pieces, though; there are lots of projects in this book that just require scraps. A single shirt can be used to make several different projects!

When you're looking at recycling your old T-shirts, there are a few ways to do it. The cotton jersey knit fabric that makes T-shirts so comfortable is stretchy and resists fraying, which makes it a great choice to refashion, to cut into panels and strips, and also to turn into yarn for woven, knit, or crocheted projects. Even cut into thin strips, it's strong and easy to work with, and it's a way of using up shirts destined for the trash in unexpected ways. Several of the projects you'll find in this book call for a skein of T-Shirt Yarn—that is, a long, continuous strip of T-shirt fabric. Learning the quick way to cut a skein from the body of a T-shirt with a few targeted cuts will turn a shirt into a continuous skein of yarn in about 10 minutes.

When choosing the T-shirt that you'll use to make your yarn, choose a T-shirt without side seams whenever

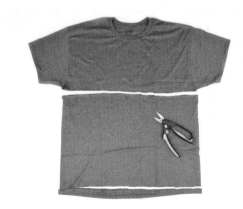

2. Fold the panel in half vertically, so that the right and left sides of the original shirt line up. Rotate the panel so that the sides of the shirt face toward you. Beginning 1" from the edge of the shirt, cut vertically from the bottom to 1" from the top of the

folded panel. Continue making these vertical cuts 1" apart—unless your project calls for a different width of fabric. You can use this process to cut a continuous strip or panel in any width.

3 Unfold your panel. You will have strips of fabric that are still intact in the center.

4 Now, cut along the top layer only, making diagonal cuts, so that you're connecting one cut strip to the neighboring strip. It's all right to have those slight corners; if you're using yarn to weave, knit, or crochet, it will stretch and roll slightly, and those corners won't show in your finished project.

5 Moving the top layer of strips out of the way, or flipping your panel over, cut vertical lines in the bottom layer, connecting the initial cuts. The end result will be one, long, continuous string—which you can now wind into a ball to use as yarn in the projects throughout the book.

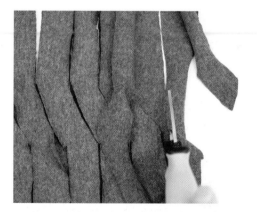

T-SHIRT TIPS!

Be sure to invest in a good, sharp pair of scissors for recycling your old tees—a spring-loaded pair is even better for reducing fatigue in your hands.

PART 1

JEWELRY AND SCARVES

Confession: I'm an accessory addict. I love having that little extra something to add to an outfit each day. If this sounds like you, you're in the right place. Here you'll learn how to make everything from bracelets to infinity scarves to necklaces, and everything in between! Repurposing a T-shirt is especially great for the projects in this part because the stretchy jersey fabric makes these beautiful items so comfortable to wear. Best of all, you'll be able to turn one shirt into several projects, so pick your favorite color and get those scissors ready!

The jersey fabric in T-shirts makes for great jewelry cord, because it's soft with a little bit of stretch—just like your favorite tee. This bracelet design may look intricate, but it doesn't involve any special weaving techniques! It's just a basic braid, with a few well-placed accent beads that give it the wow factor it needs to look like a boutique piece.

Materials

3 strips of 1"-wide T-shirt fabric, 18" long each

Flat-nosed jewelry pliers

2 crimp-on ribbon ends

15–20 large-hole metal spacer beads (with an interior hole of at least 2 millimeters)

Scissors

2 (7-millimeter) jump rings

1 (18-millimeter) lobster clasp

Optional, but helpful: Bead reamer or toothpick

1 Take your fabric strips, and lay them down on top of one another. Find the center point of the strips, then fold them in half, to create 6 strands of 9" each. Then, use your pliers to crimp a ribbon end onto the fold, making sure that all 3 strips are securely within the teeth of the ribbon end.

2 Separate your strands into 3 sections of 2 strands each.

3 Begin braiding, adding a bead to one of your two strands each time you pull one of the three sections to the center—by adding it to the same strand each time, your piece will be more uniform from start to finish. If your beads have especially small holes, you may find that you need the aid of a bead reamer, toothpick, or other small tool to press the fabric through the hole to get it started. Then you can pull it from the other end to add the bead. It's normal for it to be a tight fit! Once you get the first bead on, the rest will be easier as the cord stretches. The strand that gets stretched by adding beads will get thinner, but the other strand will stay fluffy, keeping the width the same from start to finish. The exact number of beads you need will depend on how tightly you form your braid; a looser braid will require fewer beads.

4 When you have braided for a length of 7", gather all the ends together tightly, and use your scissors to cut them so they're even. Crimp the other ribbon end on with your pliers, making sure all edges are tucked into the crimp before closing it securely.

T-SHIRT TIPS!

When choosing your beads, try mixing different shapes and textures of beads in the same color family. Using beads that are approximately the same size, but different in other ways, adds interest without detracting from the overall style.

5 Finally, twist open your jump rings with your jewelry pliers, and attach them to both ends of the bracelet. On one of your rings, add the lobster clasp before twisting the ring closed again to finish your bracelet.

Bracelets with several layers give you the stacked look in just one piece, which makes them easy to wear and to store. This project contrasts metal tube beads with T-Shirt Yarn, creating an easy and stylish accessory. No one will ever know you made it out of your favorite old shirt!

Materials

Large-eye beading needle
10 strips of ½"-wide T-shirt fabric, 8" long each
10 (2") tube beads
1 strip of ½"-wide T-shirt fabric, 6" long
Scissors
Jewelry glue
2 (10-millimeter) glue-on end caps
Ruler
2 (7-millimeter) jump rings
Flat-nosed jewelry pliers
1 (8-millimeter) lobster clasp

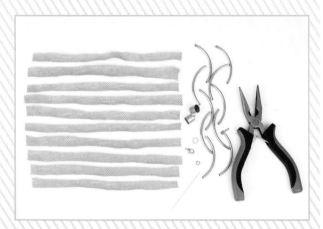

1 Thread the large-eye beading needle with your fabric strip, and string the tube beads onto the fabric. The beading needle is flexible enough that it will bend going through the tube bead. The fabric is likely to stretch as you do this, which is normal.

T-SHIRT TIPS!

Don't have a beading needle large enough for your fabric strips? A 4" piece of 26-gauge wire, twisted around the end of the fabric strip, can be used in a pinch.

2 Gather the ends of the fabric strips on the left side of the bracelet, and tie them tightly with the strip of 6" T-shirt fabric. Trim the ends of your fabric strips up evenly, close to where you tied off the bracelet end, and also cut any excess tails from the fabric strip itself. This knot only needs to last long enough to glue on the end cap, so you don't need to worry about leaving long tails or about the knot coming undone with normal wear. Then add a few drops of jewelry glue to your end cap, and glue the ends and the knot into the end cap, all together.

4 Arrange the tube beads as needed to position them at the center part of the bracelet, because it's likely that they will have shifted as you created your piece. Finally, twist open your jump rings with your jewelry pliers, and attach them to both ends of the bracelet. On one of your rings, add the lobster clasp before twisting the ring closed again to finish your bracelet.

3 Measure along your bracelet, and tie another scrap in a knot at a length of 7". Cut it off and glue the other cap, just as you did for the first one. Seven inches of fabric will make up a 7½" bracelet, which is a typical size for a ladies' bracelet. If your wrist is larger or smaller than average, feel free to make adjustments for a custom fit.

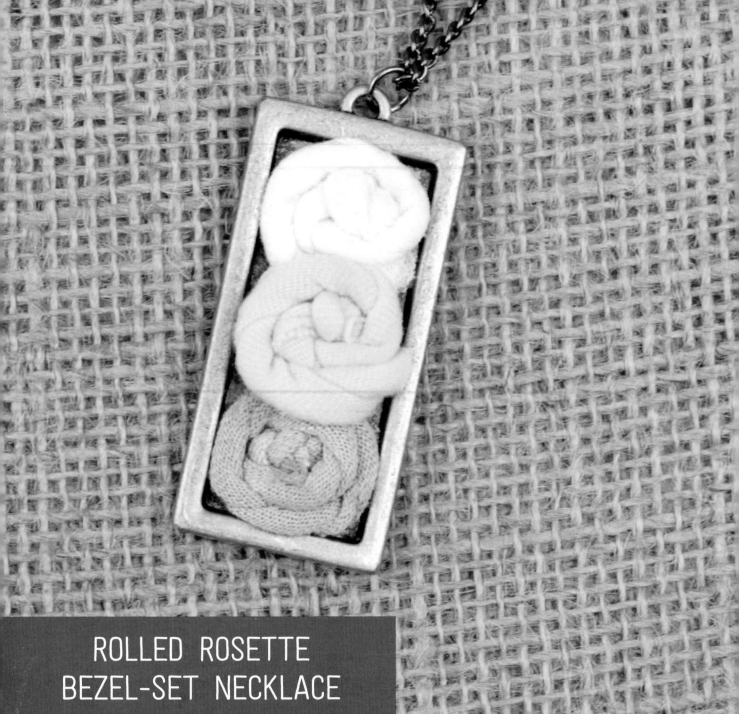

ROLLED ROSETTE
BEZEL-SET NECKLACE

These easy rolled rosettes are framed by a metal bezel, which both supports and defines this simple pendant. Choose a monochromatic color scheme, go for an *ombré* effect, or even use your team's colors for this pretty accessory. Personalizing this piece just makes it all the more unique!

Materials

3 strips of ½"-wide T-shirt fabric, 6" long each, in any color scheme you like

3 circles of T-shirt fabric, ½" in diameter, one each in colors that match your fabric strips

Fabric glue

Jewelry glue

1 (½" × ¾") rectangular jewelry bezel

1 (7-millimeter) jump ring

Flat-nosed jewelry pliers

18" chain with clasp

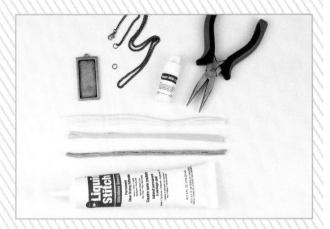

1   Tie a knot at the end of one of your strips of fabric to create the center of your rosette.

2   Gently twist the fabric strip, and wind it around the center knot. Add dots of fabric glue as you go to help secure it.

3   When your rosette is between ½" and ¾" across, cut a ½" scrap of the same fabric, and cover it with fabric glue. Glue it to the back of your rosette, taking care to tuck in the loose end. Fabric glue dries fairly quickly, but not so quickly that you are stuck with your first arrangement. If you need to rearrange any of the "petals" as you go, you can. Repeat for the next two rosettes.

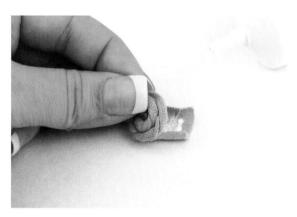

4   Decide on your arrangement, and then add a bit of jewelry glue to the bezel. Arrange the rosettes.

5   Twist open the jump ring with your jewelry pliers, and attach it to your bezel, twisting it closed. Finally, string it on a coordinating chain to finish your piece.

BRAIDED CHAIN
STATEMENT NECKLACE

The statement necklace is exactly what it sounds like: an eye-catching piece, meant to get you noticed! This braided floral design is a great casual addition to your favorite T-shirt. And, if you're just getting started making your own jewelry, this is a great beginner project because it doesn't require any special tools or techniques. If you can braid and use glue, you can jump right in with this piece.

Materials

12 yards of 1" T-Shirt Yarn (see the "How to Make T-Shirt Yarn" instructions earlier in the book)

Scissors

1 (2" × 4") coordinating rectangular fabric scrap

Fabric glue

6 strips of T-shirt fabric, 8" long each, in coordinating colors, for rosettes

1 Take the 12 yards of T-Shirt Yarn and cut it into 3 strips of 12' each. Gather the strips together and tie a knot as close to one end as possible, tying them together. Braid them into a single long braid. Tie a second knot when you reach the end. Trim the tails close to each knot.

T-SHIRT TIPS!

Keep in mind that when you braid you will lose some length; 12' lengths of yarn generally become about 9' of finished braid. However, if your yarn stretches considerably and your braid comes out a lot longer, you can either cut it off at 9' long or add an additional layer to the necklace. Each shirt will yield yarn that stretches a little differently. A necklace an inch or two short or longer won't make a significant difference.

2 Next, take the piece of 2" × 4" fabric and add a line of fabric glue to one of the long sides. Roll the fabric around to form a tube, gluing the raw edges together.

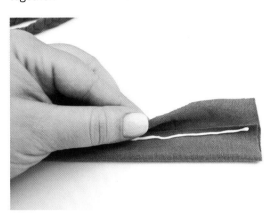

3 Next, wind the braid into loops that are approximately 36" long, being careful not to twist the braid as you work. At the point where the two ends meet, lay the knots at each end of the braid, end to end. Then, take the fabric tube that you created in the previous step, cover it liberally with fabric glue on the seam side, and wrap it snugly around the three loops of the braided yarn to cover the knots.

4 You can wear your necklace as it is, or you can add a bit of embellishment! Adding a few rolled rosettes is a pretty touch, and it also covers the seam. To make a rolled rosette, tie a knot in the end of a 6–8" piece of yarn (or any strip of fabric ½" wide). Twist the fabric gently as you wrap it in a spiral around the knot. Add a few dots of glue to the spiral as you work.

5 When you get to the size you want—a rose anywhere from ½–1" in diameter is a good size to add to this necklace—cut off any excess. From the excess, cut a small scrap of fabric the width of your rosette and glue it to the backside of the rosette to finish it.

6   Make up a few rosettes, varying the sizes and even the color for great visual variety. Attach your rosettes to the seam with fabric glue, and allow your necklace to dry overnight before wearing it.

FLORAL BIB-STYLE NECKLACE

This necklace is like a spring bouquet that never fades. Can't bear to part with team shirts, concert tees, or old shirts that belonged to someone special? Try making this bib-style necklace to keep those memories close to your heart! It's an instant update that takes an outdated, worn-out, or outgrown shirt and makes it current again.

Materials

16" necklace chain

Wire cutters

2 (10-millimeter) jump rings

Flat-nosed jewelry pliers

Needle and 8–10' of thread in a coordinating color

6 or more 1"-wide strips of T-shirt fabric or T-Shirt Yarn (see the "How to Make T-Shirt Yarn" instructions earlier in the book), between 18" and 24" long

Fabric glue

6 or more 2"-diameter fabric circles in coordinating colors (1 for each strip; diameter sizes may vary, based on your design idea)

6"-wide bib-style base

If you're using a plastic or metal bib base: jewelry glue

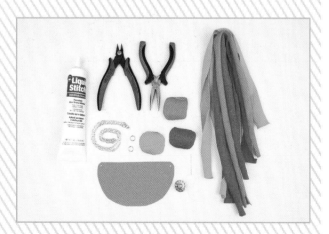

1   *To prepare the chain and bib base:* Find the center point of your necklace chain, opposite the clasp. Cut the link with your wire cutters, creating 2 8"-long chains connected by the clasp. Then, twist open the jump rings with your pliers, and attach each cut end of the chain to the holes in your bib base, twisting them closed again with your pliers.

2   *To create the roses:* Thread your needle with 12–18" of thread, and tie a knot at the bottom of one of your fabric strips in the center with your thread, securing one end directly to the fabric. Using a simple basting stitch (an over-under stitch), stitch vertically along the center of your fabric strip with ¼" stitches. It's not essential to keep these stitches uniform, so don't worry if they're a little messy—just try to keep them as close to the center of the strip as possible. You may have a shorter length of thread than your strip is long, but that's okay. When you get to the end of the fabric strip, pull the thread tight, and gather the fabric into small ruffles until your fabric strip has been reduced to about half its original length. (For example, if you started with an 18" strip, make the final length a ruffled piece 9" long.) Tie

off the thread securely at the end of the gathered fabric strip, and arrange the spacing of the ruffles as necessary.

3 Fold the ruffled strip in half along the line of stitching.

4 Roll the fabric into a spiral along the stitched edge, creating one flat side and one ruffled side.

5 Cover the flat side of your ruffled rose with fabric glue, and secure it with a fabric circle. Repeat the steps to make all six roses, or as many as you need to cover your bib base (but don't glue them to the base yet). Try varying the sizes and colors of the roses.

6 *To complete:* Decide on your arrangement, then glue the roses onto the bib base. If you're using a fiber base like chipboard or cardboard, or if your base is fabric-covered, you can complete this step using fabric glue. If you're using metal or plastic, use jewelry glue to attach the roses to the base.

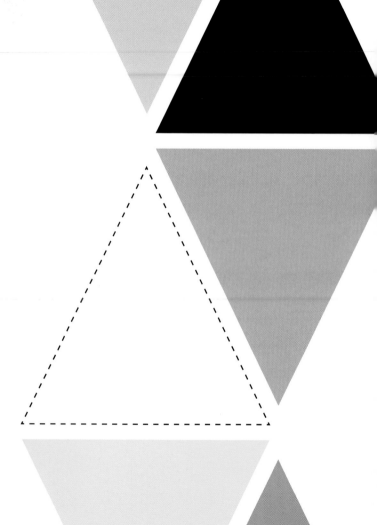

Using connectors is an easy way to incorporate found objects, repurposed items, or special focal pieces to make a bracelet. Anything with a large hole in the center, or a hole on either side, can be used as a connector. Think: washers, rings, parts from broken jewelry, specialty beads, even watch faces—you can recycle more than just a T-shirt when you make this project!

Materials

2 strips of 1½"-wide fabric, 9" long each
Focal connector of your choice
Ruler
Scissors
Jewelry pliers
2 (½") crimp-on ribbon ends
2 (7-millimeter) jump rings
1 (8-millimeter) lobster clasp

1   Double one of your fabric strips, and press the fold through your connector from the front to the back to create a loop.

2   Pass the tails of the fabric through the loop you created, and pull the tails snug, creating a lark's head knot. This type of knot is great for jewelry because it's strong and looks nice when it's finished. Take the second fabric strip and repeat the process on the other side.

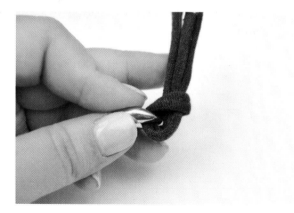

3 Take your ruler and measure your bracelet. You want the length to measure 7½" from one end to the other. If the fabric strips are too long, trim the ends, making sure that both strips are the same length. Then, use your jewelry pliers to crimp ribbon ends securely on each end of the fabric strips.

4 Finally, use your jewelry pliers to twist open the jump rings, and attach them to each end of the bracelet. On one of your rings, add the lobster clasp before twisting the ring closed again to finish your bracelet.

This woven bracelet is much simpler to make than it looks, and requires only basic jewelry-making supplies. Try making it in all one color for a monochromatic look, or mix many colors together as you use up your scraps! It's soft and stretchy, making it a comfortable piece to wear all day, and the casual look is great for a day out.

Materials

9 strips of T-shirt fabric, 1" or ½" wide and 10" long each, in your choice of colors

Scissors

Flat-nosed jewelry pliers

2 (½") crimp-on ribbon ends

Optional: Fabric glue

2 (6-millimeter) jump rings

1 (12-millimeter) lobster clasp

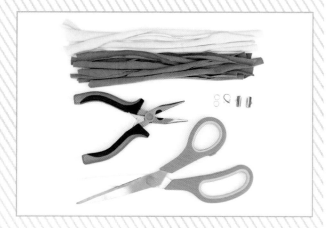

1 Take your 9 strips of T-shirt fabric and divide them into 3 groups of 3, in whatever color combinations you'd like. Next, make a knot in the end of 3 strands, leaving very short tails. Stretch your yarn to lengthen it, and braid a length of 9" (longer is fine, because you can easily cut the excess off). Then, tie an overhand knot to finish the braid. Repeat for the remaining strips until you have 3 braided strands.

T-SHIRT TIPS!

You will get a different look by choosing different ways to mix your colors! Get a color-blocked effect by braiding three of the same color strands together, then mixing different colored braids. Or create a more uniform pattern by making each braid the same as all the others. To get the look pictured, create one braid that's all gray, one braid with 2 strands of gray and 1 in aqua, and the third braid with 1 strand of gray and 2 in aqua.

2 Hold your braids together tightly, and cut off the knots. Use your flat-nosed pliers to crimp a ribbon end to the unknotted ends of each of the braids.

4 Use your jewelry pliers to twist open the jump rings, then add one to each of the ribbon ends. Use the pliers again to close them tightly—but not before you slip your lobster clasp onto one of the rings. Because this piece doesn't use any glue (unless you found you needed it when adding your ribbon ends), it's ready for wear as soon as the clasp is added!

3 Next, braid the 3 original braids together (this is what makes this bracelet double-braided). Just treat each braid as a strand, and when you reach a braided length of 6½ –7", cut off the ends, and use your flat-nosed pliers to crimp on your final ribbon end. If you find that your ends are unraveling before you can add the ribbon end, add a drop of fabric glue to each of the unknotted ends of the braids to hold them together before adding the ribbon end.

LOOM-KNIT COWL

If you have enough fluffy cowls and scarves, try knitting something different! While the use of the loom makes this project a bit more time-intensive than some of the others (plan a full hour for this one—something you can do during an episode of your favorite show), the texture you get from knitting makes this Loom-Knit Cowl a standout addition to your accessory collection. If you haven't knit or crocheted before, don't be intimidated! Loom knitters are designed to be used by kids, so they don't require you to learn special terms or abbreviations to follow the pattern, and you should be able to pick up the technique quickly!

Materials

1 skein of T-Shirt Yarn (see the "How to Make T-Shirt Yarn" instructions earlier in the book)

Extra large loom knitter (41 peg size, about 11" in diameter), hook tool, and blunt-end needle (these should be sold as a set)

Scissors

1 To begin, wrap your base row. To get started, secure a couple inches of yarn around the peg on the front of your loom. Then, begin wrapping your yarn around each peg so that the yarn is wound on the inside of the loom and the loop faces outward. This creates your stitches. T-Shirt Yarn is stretchy, but you don't want it to be too tight. Keep just enough tension on your yarn to keep from losing your stitches. As you work, the peg on the front of your loom serves as a placeholder. The yarn you've secured there also helps keep enough tension on your stitches, but once you've knitted a full row, you won't need to keep it attached to the loom. This peg will always mark your starting point as you work.

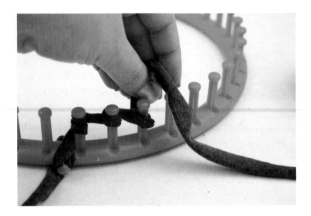

2 To knit a row, you will always be working with 2 rows of stitches. So push your first row of stiches down on the loom, and wrap a second row above it. Stop when you reach your marker peg.

4 Wrap on another row of stitches, and knit them off just as you did in the previous step. Repeat this process until your cowl has reached the size you want. Typically, one men's XL shirt will give you enough yarn to knit about 20 rows, but a larger or smaller shirt, or a blend that's stretchier, will affect the length.

3 Starting with the peg just to the left of the marker peg, use your hook tool to pick the bottom loop and pass it over the top of the peg and off the loom entirely. You will be left with just one row, allowing you to continue adding rows in the next step. Work your way to the right, until you've worked all the way around the loom. When you've finished all the pegs, you have effectively knitted a full row! And if working left to right feels awkward to you, it's perfectly acceptable to work right to left instead. It's the process that matters, not the direction.

T-SHIRT TIPS!

There's no rule that says you have to stop knitting at 20 rows. If you prefer a taller cowl that will fully cover your neck, tie two skeins of yarn together and keep knitting! You can even make stripes or color-blocked patterns by using other colors of yarn in your cowl.

5 Once you've reached your desired size, bind off the final edge of your cowl by threading the blunt-end needle onto the end of your yarn and passing the needle up through each stitch remaining on the loom, moving from the top of one stitch to the bottom of the next.

6 When you have stitched through the entire row, tie a secure knot to a loop in the bottom row to finish off your cowl. Now, trim the excess yarn, slip the cowl off the loom entirely, and tie a secure knot on the beginning end of your cowl, cutting off the excess. The edges of the cowl will roll slightly (this is normal!), which will cover up the beginning and ending knots. The finished cowl just slips easily over your head for wear!

CHAIN-EMBELLISHED
INFINITY SCARF

One of the easiest accessories to wear is the infinity scarf. All it takes is a simple wrap once or twice over your head—no knots to master, and you've got an instant accessory. An infinity scarf makes a great addition to any outfit, but because it covers the neck, you typically have to decide whether to wear your scarf or your favorite necklace. Fortunately, this project adds a chain to a basic scarf so that you don't have to choose—it's half scarf, half jewelry, and all style! Look around at what you have for broken or outdated necklaces, and reuse your old chain to make this a truly recycled accessory.

Materials

1 T-shirt
Scissors
Fabric glue
Assortment of 4 or 5 chains, between 24" and 32" long each
Optional: Fabric marker with disappearing ink
Flat-nosed jewelry pliers
2 (12-millimeter) jump rings

1 To make your scarf, you'll start with yarn created using the same technique you learned in the "How to Make T-Shirt Yarn" instructions earlier in the book. However, for this project, you need to make the yarn much wider. Remove the body panel and bottom hem from the shirt, and fold it in half vertically. Rotate the panel so that the sides of the shirt are facing you, then cut just once at the center of the panel, making a vertical cut 3" long. For the standard men's shirt, this should be at the 8" point, but as long as you cut at the center, the width isn't critical. A 7" or 9" width will also work well.

2 Open the panel to finish your cuts on the right side, cutting diagonally from the center on the edge of the panel to the cut you made at the top. On the left side, cut from the bottom cut diagonally to the center point of the left edge. On the backside of your panel, make the same vertical cut between your top and bottom cuts as you would make if you were cutting yarn—the only difference is that you only need to make one cut instead of many.

3 Remove the triangular ends from the long strip you just created, and toss them into your scrap bin. There are lots of other projects you can make where these scraps will be useful!

4 Use your fabric glue to connect the two raw edges that you just removed the triangles from together. Allow it to partially dry, about 20 minutes, before continuing.

5 Determine the points where you want to attach your chains. If you're using reclaimed chains in odd lengths, your points may vary. To figure this out, simply lay out the scarf and chains in an oblong shape, and check the positioning. If desired, you can use a marker to make a small dot to help you remember your positioning.

6 Using your jewelry pliers, twist open one of your jump rings. Add the chains to it, and then poke an end through about ½" of fabric, at the spot you just determined. Using your pliers, twist the jump ring closed again. Repeat this step at the other attachment point. It's not necessary to cover these attachment points, because as you wear the scarf the folds will come together, covering up your jump rings.

RUFFLE SCARF

This ruffled scarf is as soft and comfortable as your favorite shirt, and the ruffles give it a fun and feminine texture that adds flair to any outfit. Everyone you meet will say, "Whoa, you *made* that?" And, despite the complex look, you can complete the project just by making a few strategic cuts. Beautiful and easy—what could be better?

Materials

1 T-shirt
Scissors
Paper plate (or other 8"–9" round item to use as a tracing guide)
Marker
Fabric glue

1. Cut the sleeves away from your T-shirt, and cut the top seams open.

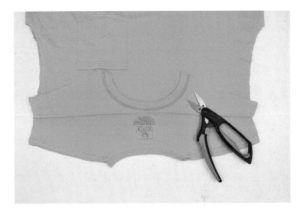

2. Using the paper plate, begin tracing circles on either side of your shirt. (You need at least 10 circles for a proper scarf, but more will give you a fuller scarf. The men's XL shirt with a pocket that I used for the scarf shown in the pictures yielded 11 circles.) Shirts with pockets aren't ideal, but if yours has one, just work around it. Don't include it in any of your circles.

3 To maximize your fabric, cut close to the circles down one side of your shirt, then trace as many circles as you can from the opened-up shirt. It may seem strange not to just cut a straight line directly down the side of the shirt, but there's wasted space (which translates to wasted shirt) any time you cut circles from a square-cut piece of fabric. You will be able to fit more circles if they are nested together, and you just may need that little bit of extra fabric to trace one or two more circles when you get to the other side of the shirt panel.

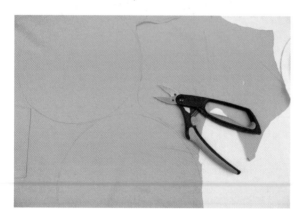

4 Next, cut your circles into spirals to create long, ruffled strips. Cut in from the edge, keeping a 2" distance between the spiral and the outer edge of the circle (or the outer cut of the spiral). You can cut more than one spiral at a time, so save time by stacking up as many as your scissors can handle! When you've cut all the spirals, take hold of them at opposite ends, and pull to stretch them. They will go from flat fabric to ruffled lengths with a simple tug.

5 Now, pair up your ruffled strips, and glue two of them together with fabric glue at the small ends— the outermost part of the spiral. If you have an even number, that's great. If you have an odd number, don't worry, you'll just have one length that doesn't get any glue.

6 Stack up the glued ruffles, and if you had an odd number of spirals, take the unglued one and tie it tightly around the group at the glued seam, securing all your glued strips together where the scarf will rest at the back of your neck. This will give you a shorter ruffle on each side of the finished scarf.

If you had an even number of spirals, raid the remnants of your original shirt, and cut a strip of fabric 2" wide by at least 6" long. It does not have to be perfectly rectangular, but it does need to be 2" wide for a strong knot. Tie this piece tightly around the group of ruffles. You can cut off the excess if it doesn't blend in. As soon as the glue dries, get ready to wow with this great accessory!

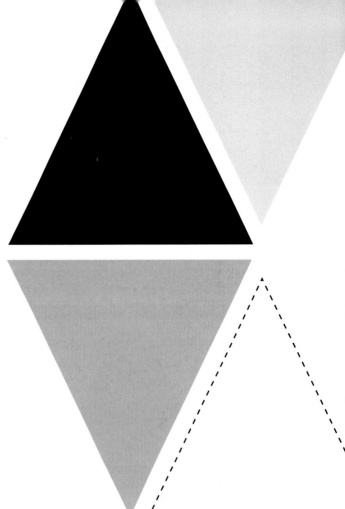

SIMPLE TASSEL SCARF

This Simple Tassel Scarf is a great, quick project that can add a pop of color to any outfit—or, in a pinch, be made up for extra warmth on an unseasonably cold day. If you have 15 minutes and a sharp pair of scissors, a few targeted cuts will transform an old shirt into a surprisingly stylish cool-weather accessory that you'll never want to take off!

Materials

1 T-shirt
Scissors

1 To make your scarf, you'll start by using the same technique for making T-Shirt Yarn that you can find in the "How to Make T-Shirt Yarn" instructions earlier in the book. However, for this project, your cuts will be much wider. Remove the body panel and bottom hem from the shirt, and fold it in half vertically. Rotate the panel so that the sides of the shirt are facing you, and make 2 shallow cuts, 4" long, 6" apart.

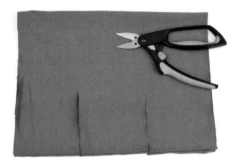

2 Open the panel to finish your cuts. Instead of having several rows to cut to finish the yarn, you will only have a few, but the process is the same. On the right side, cut diagonally from the center on the edge of the panel to the cut you made at the top. On the left side, cut from the bottom cut diagonally to the center point of the left edge. Make a diagonal cut to connect the two remaining cuts. On the opposite side of your panel, make the same vertical cut between your top and bottom cuts as you would make if you were cutting yarn—the only difference is that you only need to make two initial cuts, instead of many.

4   Double up the strips so that the scarf is thick enough, then tie an overhand knot in each end, leaving a double tail on each end of about 6" long. Cut each of the tails into several ½"-wide strips, to make fringe. Pull on each strip and it will curl slightly for a finished look. Trim up any uneven ends, and your Simple Tassel Scarf is ready to be worn!

3   Remove the triangular ends from the long strip you just created, and toss them into your scrap bin. You will be left with one long strip of 6"-wide fabric. Depending on the shirt size you used, it should be 10–12' long. Find the center point (somewhere between 5' and 6'), and cut the strip in half, creating two equal-length strips.

BRAIDED SCARF

Braids never go out of style, and this four-color scarf is lightweight and stylish, making it perfect for any time you find a little chill in the air. You can change up your color choices by season, or show your spirit by celebrating in team colors with this easy project.

Materials

4 T-shirts
Scissors

1. To create each strand of your 4-part braid, you will be using the same technique for making T-Shirt Yarn that you'll find in the "How to Make T-Shirt Yarn" instructions earlier in the book. However, for this project, you'll be making the yarn 5" wide. Remove the body panel and bottom hem from each shirt, and fold it in half vertically. Then, rotate the panel so that the sides of the shirt are facing you, and make 3 equally spaced cuts, each at about 4–5" from each other and from the edges of the fabric. (This can vary depending on the size shirt you're using, so making the cuts an equal width is more important than the exact width.)

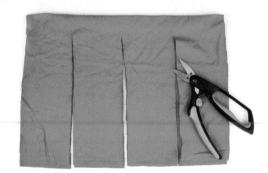

2. Open the panel to finish your cuts. On the right side, on the top layer only, cut diagonally from the center on the edge of the panel to the cut you made at the top. On the left side, cut from the bottom cut diagonally to the center point of the left edge. Make a diagonal cut to connect the two remaining cuts. On the backside of your panel, make vertical cuts between your top and bottom cuts, connecting them. Remove the triangular ends from the long strips you just created, and toss them into your scrap bin.

3 Repeat the cuts for the other 3 shirts. You may find that your strips aren't all the same lengths, but that's fine for now. You can even them up at the end.

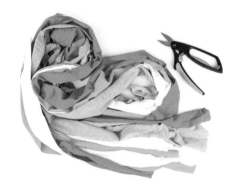

5 When you finish about 8' of braiding, tie an overhand knot in the end and trim the fabric, leaving a 6" tail. Finally, cut each of the tails into ½"-wide strips, to make fringe. Pull on each strip and it will curl slightly for a finished look. Trim up any uneven ends, and this Braided Scarf is ready to be worn!

T-SHIRT TIPS!

If you find a 4-part braid to be difficult to master, this scarf looks great as a traditional 3-part braid as well! It will be slightly less full, but you'll still get the look—with a more familiar technique.

4 Tie an overhand knot in all 4 shirts, leaving about a 6" tail. Then use the long side of the yarn to begin braiding a 4-part braid. A 4-part braid is very similar to a 3-part braid—the only difference is that as you work, you keep two of the parts instead of one on your left side. Each time you pull from the right side, you will pull that part over one section, to the center. Each time you pull from the left side, you bring that part over two other sections.

FRINGED INFINITY SCARF

This easy Fringed Infinity Scarf is something you can make in just minutes, and requires nothing but scissors and one retired shirt. The simple style and easy steps make it a great choice for a group craft or camp craft, or a perfect project for instant gratification anytime.

Materials

1 T-shirt
Scissors

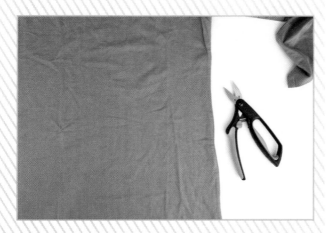

1   Cut the panel from the body of your T-shirt at the arms, and remove the bottom hem. For this project, side seams won't get in your way, so it's easy to make this scarf from either a men's or women's T-shirt. Just be sure, if you are using a shirt with side seams, that you cut out any tags that may be sewn into the seams.

2   Fold the panel in half horizontally, so that the raw edges line up, then make uniform cuts every ¼" to ½" along the raw edge, cutting 3" into the panel.

3 Pull on each strip, so that the fabric rolls slightly. This will give it a more finished look. If you have used a shirt with side seams, those fringe pieces won't roll up nicely, so it's better to cut those pieces off. The finished scarf will have fringe on both sides—the top and bottom. To wear it so that all the fringe faces down, away from your face, just roll the top edge over the bottom edge. This scarf can be worn doubled up and close to the neck, or long and loose. Your choice!

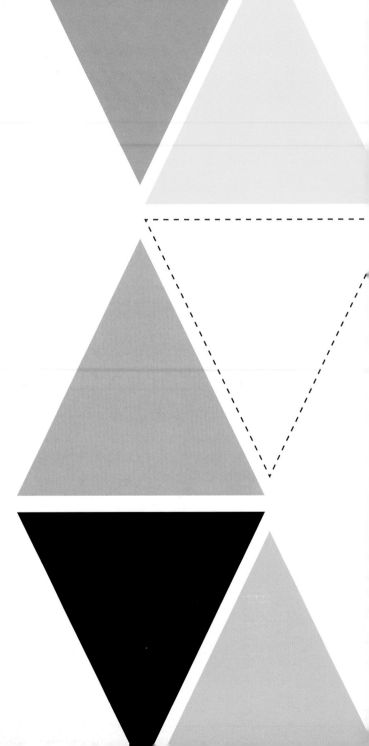

PART 2

ACCESSORIES

If you're looking for a way to glam up your wardrobe, look no further than the accessories found throughout this part! Here you'll find pretty additions to your hair, your shoes, your bags, and much more! These great DIYs have you covered from head to toe. Most of the projects here are great scrap busters, using small pieces of fabric, a bit of glue, or a needle and thread here and there. It's a great reason to save those extra sleeves and strips—so you can add a bit of color and style to your everyday favorites. Enjoy!

RHINESTONE BUTTON
BOOT CUFFS

Boot cuffs give the illusion of wearing tall socks or legwarmers under your boots by adding a cuff that tucks into just the upper part of the boot. It's much more comfortable for wear, because you don't have all that bulk tucked into your boots, but still allows you to accessorize your footwear. These boot cuffs add a little sparkle, and the lightweight fabric is nice for warmer weather. You just need a pair of T-shirt sleeves to make your cuffs, and you can embellish them to match any outfit.

Materials

2 sleeves from a men's short-sleeved T-shirt
Fabric glue
6 rhinestone buttons
Needle and 24–36" of thread
Scissors

1 Determine the width your cuffs should be by measuring the cuff around your calf with leggings or tights, and folding the excess over to create a new seam based on your measurement. Since not all bodies are the same size, making your own cuffs is a great way to get a great fit! Remember, there is some stretch to T-shirt fabric, so fit it snugly against your calf.

2 Arrange the seam on the edge of the sleeve to ensure that you are left with a straight tube, rather than a sleeve that is wider at one end and narrower at the other. Fold from this edge to resize the cuff to fit your calf. Use the sleeve's hem as a straight line along the top, to guide you in creating this new seam.

3 Glue this new seam down with fabric glue to secure it. Be sure to add a bit of glue on the inside of the seam, too.

T-SHIRT TIPS!

If you aren't handy with a needle and thread, gluing small fabric flowers on instead of rhinestones will also give you a great look—with no sewing necessary. Just make sure you secure the seam with plenty of fabric glue.

4 Sew rhinestone buttons onto the top half of the cuff to help cover the seam, and to add some sparkle! Sewing through to the other side will also help to reinforce the seam. If rhinestones really aren't your thing, feel free to choose something that better matches your personal style. Then, cut the bottom of the cuff off so that the bottom edge is straight, and tuck the cuffs into your favorite boots for an instant fashion upgrade!

DRAPED VEST

The draped vest is one of the easiest accessories you can make from a T-shirt. It's worn halter-style, so it can be made from just one shirt, and layered over your favorite tee. You just need 5 minutes and a pair of scissors to make your own great accessory! Women's shirts work as well as men's for this project, since you'll be removing any side seams from the shirt.

Materials

1 T-shirt
Scissors

1 Remove the bottom hem from your shirt, and then cut all along the two sides, through both layers, removing the side seam (if there is one) and the sleeves.

2 Cutting through both layers, completely remove the neckline from the shirt. For crew-neck styles, it will probably be necessary to cut a hole a little larger than the neckline.

3 Turn the vest horizontal for wear, and put both arms through the hole that was once the neck. One shoulder of the former shirt will be the halter-style neck strap, and the other will rest across the back. The front and back panels of the shirt become the draped front.

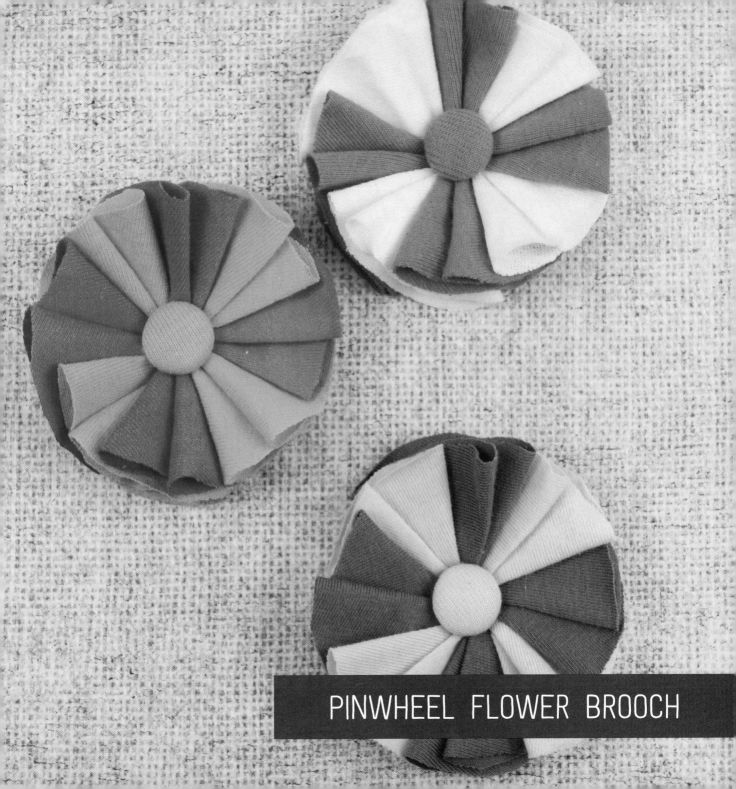

PINWHEEL FLOWER BROOCH

You may think brooches are out of date, but you don't have to pin one to your lapel to accessorize. Fastening a bright, springy flower to a plain tote, hat, or scarf is a great way to add a pop of color without locking into the look permanently. Brooches and pins can even be added to plain home décor pieces, too! This Pinwheel Flower Brooch is fun to make, and if you're raiding your scrap bin to make it, then it will already match some of your other DIY projects.

Materials

8 (2½"-diameter) circles, in 2 colors
Fabric glue
Needle and 12–18" of coordinating thread
2 (2"-diameter) circles in one of your two colors, for the brooch base
2 (1¼"-diameter) circles in a coordinating color, for the button
⅝" size fabric button maker set
Jewelry glue
Brooch/pin base

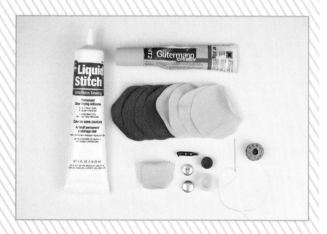

1 Fold your 2½" circles into quarters. Add fabric glue to the back of one of the 2" circles, then press on the quartered circles, using an overlapping pinwheel pattern and alternating the colors.

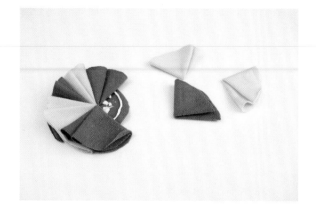

2 Using your needle and thread, sew around the center of your pinwheel. Be sure to go through every set of petals. This stitching doesn't need to be perfect; it just needs to help secure your petals together and be small enough to be covered up by the button center.

3   Make your coordinating fabric-covered button. To do this, center your 2 (1¼") fabric circles over the button maker base, and use the button cap to press them down. Then, add the button back and press again.

undo a piece that's glued shut. Allow your glue to dry, and then see what you can do with a modern-day brooch!

T-SHIRT TIPS!

Your button maker will come with detailed instructions, so if you are new to fabric-covered buttons, don't be intimidated! Fabric buttons are very easy to make, and once you make a few, you'll love adding them to all kinds of projects.

4   Sew the button onto the center of the pinwheel, and glue the remaining 2" circle to the back of the flower with fabric glue, to give it more support.

5   Using the jewelry glue, adhere the brooch base to the back of the flower. Be especially careful with your glue on each end of the metal base, near the moving parts. If glue drips over the edges, you risk gluing your pin closed. You can always add a little more glue later if you need more hold, but you can't

FLORAL SHOE CLIPS

Do you have a pair of plain flats in your closet that could use a little brightening up? Then these Floral Shoe Clips are for you! Making a pair of shoe clips (or a few pairs!) is a fun and easy way to give new life to your favorite old shoes, without altering them permanently. Match multiple outfits with a pair of comfortable neutral shoes and colorful sets of DIY shoe clips—because recycling your scraps for a new look is much easier on the budget than buying new.

Materials

Needle and 12–18" of coordinating thread
2 strips of 1"-wide T-shirt fabric, 24" long each
Fabric glue
2 (2"-diameter) fabric circles
Jewelry glue
2 (1½"-long) alligator-style hair clips

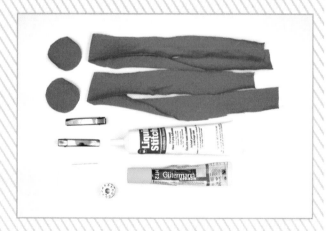

1 Thread your needle with 12–18" of thread, sew it through the center of one of your fabric strips, at a short end, and then knot the end of the thread, securing it to the end of the fabric strip. Using a simple basting stitch (pushing the needle over and under the cloth), stitch vertically with ¼" stitches along the center of your fabric strip. It's not essential to keep these stitches uniform, so don't worry if they're a little messy—just try to keep them as close to the center of the strip as possible. You may have a shorter length of thread than your strip is long, but that's okay. When you get to the end of the fabric strip, pull the thread tight and gather the fabric into small ruffles until your fabric strip has been reduced to about half its original length. (For example, if you started with an 18" strip, make the final length a ruffled piece 9" long.) Tie off the thread securely at the end of the gathered fabric strip and arrange the ruffles as necessary to distribute them evenly.

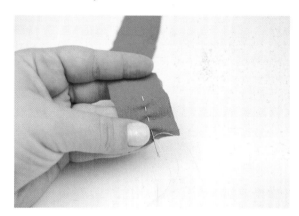

2 Fold the ruffled strip in half along the line of stitching.

3 Roll the fabric into a spiral along the stitched edge. This will create one flat side and one ruffled side.

4 Cover the flat side of your ruffled rose with fabric glue, and secure it with a fabric circle.

5 Add a line of jewelry glue to the top side of one your hair clips, and add the rose to the clip. Be sure to cover the clip hinge with the rose, to keep it from showing.

6 Repeat these steps to create the second clip.

7 Allow the clips to dry at least an hour before wearing, and then you can add them not just to shoes but to bags, your hair, your home décor, and more!

ROLLED ROSETTE
HAIR PINS

Floral accents work for almost every style, and these simple pins are a fun way to hold your hair in place. What's even better is that they are easy—and fast—to make! They only take a couple of basic supplies, and they use so little fabric that you'll be able to make them from just about any piece you find in your scrap bin. So dive in, whip up these tiny floral rosettes, and enjoy the instant gratification!

Materials

2 strips of ½"-wide T-shirt fabric, 6" long each
Fabric glue
2 scraps of T-shirt fabric large enough to cover your rosette bases
Jewelry glue
2 hair pins with glue pads
1 scrap of any fabric (for use when setting glue to dry)

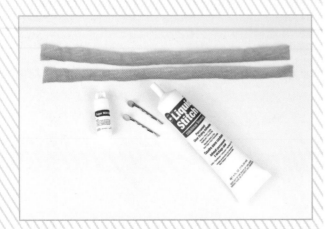

1 Tie a knot at the end of a piece of fabric to create the center of your rosette.

2 Gently twist the fabric strip, and wind it around the center knot. Add dots of fabric glue as you go, to help secure it.

3 When your rosette is about ½" in diameter (or whatever size best fits your style), cut a scrap of fabric the same width, and cover it with fabric glue. Glue it to the back of your rosette, taking care to tuck in the loose end. Fabric glue dries fairly quickly, but not so quickly that you are stuck with your first

arrangement. If you need to rearrange any of the "petals" as you go, you can.

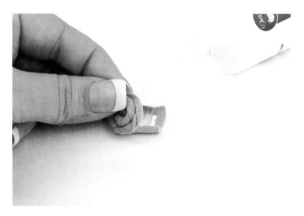

4 Add a drop of jewelry glue to the glue pad on your hair pin, and glue the rosette to it. To be sure it doesn't detach or shift while drying, lay the hair pin with the rosette side facing down and prop up the other end with a scrap of fabric to keep it level. Repeat the steps for the second pin. Try to match the size of the first rosette as closely as possible.

If you have long hair, or have a girl in the house who does, put this project on your must-make list. This simple barrette is fun, feminine, and really easy to create. It's a great place to start if you're just jumping into making your own accessories because it doesn't take much in the way of supplies, and you only need one finished rosette to make it look great!

Materials

Needle and 12–18" of coordinating thread
1 strip of 1"-wide T-shirt fabric, 18" long
Fabric glue
1 (1½") fabric circle
Jewelry glue
Barrette base

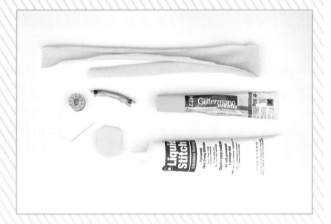

1 Thread your needle with 12–18" of thread, and tie a knot at the bottom of your fabric strip in the center, securing it to the end of the fabric strip. Using a simple basting stitch (an over-under stitch), stitch vertically with ¼" stitches along the center of your fabric strip. It's not essential to keep these stitches uniform, so don't worry if they're a little messy—just try to keep them as close to the center of the strip as possible. You may have a shorter length of thread than your strip is long, but that's okay.

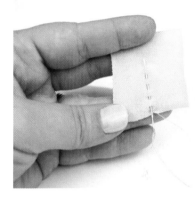

2 When you get to the end of the fabric strip, pull the thread tight and gather the fabric into small ruffles until your fabric strip has been reduced to about half its original length. (For example, if you started with an 18" strip, make the final length a ruffled piece 9" long.) Tie off the thread securely at the end of the gathered fabric strip, then fold the ruffled strip in half along the line of stitching and arrange the ruffles as necessary to distribute them evenly.

4 Using jewelry glue, attach the ruffled rose to the barrette base. Allow it to dry fully, for at least an hour, before wearing.

3 Roll the fabric into a spiral along the stitched edge. This will create one flat side and one ruffled side. Add a line of fabric glue all along your stitched line, and glue the fabric circle to the back.

If you're looking for an easy and colorful way to keep your hair back from your face during your workout, cleaning spree, day at the beach, or anytime at all, it doesn't get better than this headband with a twist. It's a little more sophisticated than just tying a fabric strip on your head, but it's nearly as simple—and the stretchy T-shirt fabric will hold your hair in place, guaranteed!

Materials

1 strip of 3"-wide T-shirt fabric, 22" long
Fabric glue

1   *To make:* All you have to do is glue one raw edge to the other! Lay out the fabric strip on a flat surface, making sure it isn't twisted. Then, put fabric glue on the edge of one of the short ends, and glue it to the other edge of the strip. Allow it to dry at least an hour before wearing.

2   *To wear:* Open the head band as a circle, and position the seam edge off to one side. Twist it twice in the center, creating a figure-8.

3 Then, fold the 2 sides over so the fabric is doubled up, and your Easy Twisted Headband is ready to wear.

The sailor knot is a classic nautical design that looks much more complicated than it actually is. Once you give this project a try, you will want to make one up in every color! Even a bad hair day can get a boost with this cute and colorful hair accessory.

Materials

20' of T-Shirt Yarn (see the "How to Make T-Shirt Yarn" instructions earlier in the book)

Scissors

Ruler

1 (3" × 3") square of fabric in the same color as your T-Shirt Yarn

Fabric glue

1 Cut the yarn into 10 pieces, 2' long each. Separate them into 2 groups of 5 pieces each. Line up the strips in the first group neatly side by side, and make one loop with all 5 pieces, with the tail ends facing down. Overlap the left tails over the right tails.

2 Line up the second group of pieces side by side, grouping them together as you did with the first 5 pieces. Wrap them around the existing loop in a U shape. Pass this U shape under the right "leg" of tails in your first group and over the left leg.

3 Pass the left "arm" of the U shape under the original loop, bringing it to the right.

4 Weave the right arm of the U-shape over the loop, under the left arm of the U-shape, and then over the other side of the original loop. You will now have a loose but complete knot that resembles a figure-8 shape.

5 Tighten the knot, and adjust it as necessary.

6 Measure your headband from end to end, and cut it to a total length of 22", making all the ends an even length. Cover your 3" fabric piece liberally with fabric glue, and place the strands on the glue-covered fabric square end to end. Take a moment to add glue between the strands as well, so that they will all be secured to each other as well as the fabric square, then wrap the ends with the fabric square. Allow the headband to dry overnight before wearing it.

If you love roses and want an easy way to wear them in your hair, this larger ruffled rose is a surprisingly realistic-looking fabric flower. This headband sports a single rose that's a great look for short hair, up-dos, and even for baby girls, if you use a more age-appropriate stretchy headband as your base.

Materials

Needle and 12–18" of coordinating thread
1 strip of 2½"-wide T-shirt fabric, 18" long
2 (1½"-diameter) fabric circles
Fabric glue
1 coordinating headband
Jewelry glue

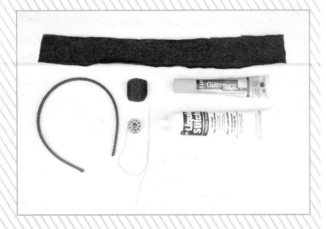

1   Thread your needle with 12–18" of thread, and tie a knot at the bottom of your fabric strip in the center, securing it to the end of the fabric strip. Using a simple basting stitch (an over-under stitch), stitch vertically using ¼" stitches along the center of your fabric strip. It's not essential to keep these stitches uniform, so don't worry if they're a little messy— just try to keep them as close to the center of the strip as possible. You may have a shorter length of thread than your strip is long, but that's okay.

2 When you get to the end of the fabric strip, pull the thread tight and gather the fabric into small ruffles until your fabric strip measures 12". Tie off the thread securely at the end of the gathered fabric strip, and arrange the ruffles as necessary to distribute them evenly along the thread.

3 Fold the ruffled strip in half along the line of stitching.

4 Roll the fabric into a spiral along the stitched edge. This will create one flat side and one ruffled side. Cover the flat side of your ruffled rose with fabric glue, and secure it with a fabric circle.

5 Position your rose along the headband so it's offset to one side, and put jewelry glue on both the back of the rose and your second fabric circle. Sandwich the headband securely between the 2 fabric circles, and allow it to dry overnight.

BRAIDED LANYARD

If you wear a badge for work or for play, or you carry your keys without pockets or a purse, chances are you know how convenient a lanyard can be! But just because it's functional doesn't mean you have to settle for plain. If you have a few feet of T-Shirt Yarn left on a ball or two, you can make your own lanyard, in colors you love.

Materials

4 lengths of T-Shirt Yarn, 4' long each, in various colors (see the "How to Make T-Shirt Yarn" instructions earlier in the book)

2 (½") crimp-on ribbon ends

Flat-nosed jewelry pliers

Optional: Fabric glue

2 (7-millimeter) split jump rings

Hinged swivel clasp

1. Choose 4 stands of yarn, gather them together at the ends, and use your pliers to crimp a ribbon end tightly onto all 4 gathered ends.

2. Now begin creating a 4-part braid. A 4-part braid is very similar to a 3-part braid—the only difference is that as you work, you keep two of the parts instead of one on your left side. Each time you pull from the right side, you will pull that part over one section, to the center.

3 As you pull from the left side, bring that part over the two left-most sections to the center.

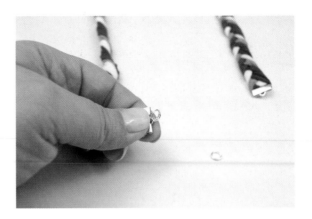

4 When you have braided a length between 42" and 48", it's time to finish the ends and assemble. Hold the end of your braid tightly, cut off any uneven ends, and crimp on the second ribbon end. If you find it difficult to get all the ends into the ribbon end, you can add a few drops of fabric glue to hold it together while you crimp on the finished end. Now, just add your jump rings to the ribbon ends. The best type of rings to use are those that can withstand heavy use, because a lanyard is the type of thing that will occasionally catch on something or get tugged as you go about your day. A split ring is ideal for this type of daily abuse—it's a double ring, like a key ring, only jewelry-sized. For each jump ring, just pry one side open wide enough to slide it onto a ribbon end.

5 Finally, attach the base of the swivel clasp to the split rings to finish your lanyard. The hinge on your swivel clasp will allow you to easily add or remove your card or keys each day!

T-SHIRT TOTE BAG

It only takes about 20 minutes to totally transform a T-shirt into a practical tote bag! T-shirt totes are a great green choice when you're out shopping, and they're also a perfect way to keep and show off those favorite tees from concerts and events that you may not wear often (or . . . ever) but still feel nostalgic about, and don't want to get rid of. This project can be made with minimal hand sewing to reinforce the bottom seam, but if you're handy with a sewing machine, one line of stitching gives you an instant tote.

Materials

1 T-shirt
Scissors
24–30" of ⅝" iron-on seam adhesive
Iron
Needle and 3–4' of coordinating embroidery floss

1 Fold the shirt in half vertically down the center, then cut off the arms and neck opening.

2 Unfold the shirt and rotate it so your newly made handles (the former shoulders of the original shirt) line up. Cut off the bottom hem of the shirt, curving the bottom edge slightly.

3 Cut a length of seam adhesive the same width as your tote. Iron on the seam adhesive along the bottom edge of the tote, and allow it to cool fully. Each brand will have slightly different instructions, so check the package for your exact brand, but it should only take a few seconds to fuse the

adhesive. Then, remove the paper backing, line up the edges of your fabric, and iron again, fusing the seam together. It will strengthen as it cools, so don't put any stress on the warm seam.

groceries, over time you'll need mor[e] adhesive to maintain the seam's int[e...]

4 Finally, use the embroidery floss to sew a basic whip stitch—a wide stitch that you add in a spiral—along the bottom seam of your tote. It's primarily decorative, but it will also help to reinforce the strength of the seam, in case you carry heavy items in your bag from time to time. If you're just carrying gym clothes or something lightweight, the stitching isn't necessary, but if you want to tote books or

GALAXY BLEACHED
NO-SEW TOTE BAG

This great tote is as fun to design and create as it is to carry when you hit up the gym or the farmers' market. A few cuts and a spray bottle of bleach will transform an old tee into this unique celestial-themed bag—no sewing required!

Materials

1 T-shirt

Scissors

Freezer paper

Iron

1–2 ounces of liquid chlorine bleach in a spray bottle

Fabric glue

1. Cut the body panel away from the shirt at the arms. About 3" from the hem, cut a handle that's ½" wide by 5–6" long, through both layers of fabric. Then, from the upper part of the shirt, cut an additional strip of fabric 3" wide and approximately 18" long. Set this strip aside, as you will be using it in the final step.

2. Draw or trace stars of varying sizes onto the paper side (not the waxed side) of your freezer paper, then cut out the stars. Using a medium-high setting without steam, iron the stars onto your tote panel with the paper side up and the waxy side facing the shirt panel, to create instant, temporary stencils.

3 Next, tape your tote panel to a vertical surface and spray it with bleach. It's best if you can do this step either outside or in a space that's easy to wipe down, like the inside of your shower. Be very careful not to get the bleach on yourself, your clothing, your upholstery, or any other fibers, or you will bleach them, too. A little goes a long way, so spray from a distance, and wait a minute between sprays to allow the fabric to lighten up. This is a very forgiving design, so if you accidentally soak an area with bleach, it won't be obvious. Leave some areas unbleached, especially near the edges and near the tape holding up your panel, or they will look like obvious seams when you're finished. You can always rotate the tote panel to bleach additional areas after you finish one section if you want to lighten up the whole design. If you want the bleached areas to be even lighter, wait about 30 minutes until the shirt dries before giving them a second pass because the bleached areas will continue to lighten as they dry.

4 Allow your shirt to dry for at least 30 minutes, then peel off your stencils. You may find that they begin to peel off on their own as they dry, and that's fine. The wax creates a temporary bond, which makes it easy to remove, and it also leaves no residue behind. Finish your tote by gathering the cut bottom edge in one hand and adding fabric glue to the folds created. The glue will help strengthen the bottom of the tote.

5 Before the glue dries, tie your fabric strip tightly around the gathered base of the tote. To make it more decorative, you can tie the strip in a bow, or trim the ends to a few inches and cut them into fringe. Allow the glue to dry for at least 30 minutes before using your new tote.

T-SHIRT TIPS!

Freezer paper is a specialty paper you can find in your grocery aisle alongside aluminum foil and other kitchen wraps. One side is paper and the other has a waxy coating, allowing it to be ironed onto fabric to create stencils with a temporary, mess-free bond. It's unlike wax paper, which is waxed on both sides (and will leave wax on your iron), and also different from parchment paper, which has no wax to adhere your cutouts to your project. If freezer paper isn't available where you live, you may have success using butcher paper instead, or try using craft vinyl or contact paper to create your stencils. Also, if you own an electronic or manual cutting machine, you can also die-cut your freezer paper, making this project even quicker and easier to complete!

Make your trip to the parking meter or the laundry just a little happier by turning your favorite old tee into a custom coin purse! This little purse would be especially fun made from a shirt with a chest emblem, to show off your personal style. And, if you're handy with a needle and thread, you can easily substitute a sew-in purse frame available in most local craft stores for the glue-in version listed here. I had to do a quick Google search to order a glue-in purse frame online, but it was well worth the time saved not to hand-stitch the purse together.

Materials

2 (4" × 8") rectangles of T-shirt fabric
32" of ⅝" iron-on seam adhesive
Iron
Scissors
1 (3" × 1½") glue-in purse frame
Jewelry glue

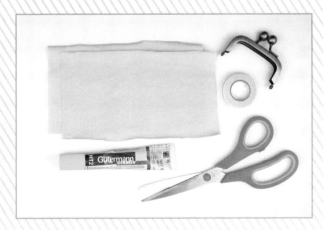

1 Iron your seam adhesive onto each of the 4 edges of the back (if there is a difference between the front and back) of one fabric rectangle. Then, remove the paper backing, line up the edges of your fabric, and iron the second panel onto the first. Adding adhesive all the way around the edge of your fabric will make the pouch of your purse stronger by providing a second layer, and it will also stiffen your edges, which will help you glue the frame on later.

2 Add a 3½" strip of adhesive along each of the long edges of one side of your layered rectangle from the center of the rectangle to ½" from the edge; if your purse is going to have an outer design, do this on what will be the outside of the purse. Fold the rectangle in half, forming a basic pouch, and iron the sides closed. Allow the adhesive to cool fully before continuing, which should only take 1–2 minutes.

3 Trim any uneven edges, turn the pouch right-side out, and iron it as flat as possible.

4 Separate the 2 layers at the opening to 1½". (If you're using a different size purse frame, separate your layers by the same amount as the height of your frame.) Chances are, your frame has rounded corners, so you will need to round the top edges of your fabric to match it.

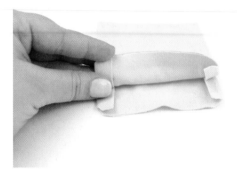

5 Add glue to the inside of one side of the purse frame, and carefully insert the fabric. Allow it to dry enough to be secure, which should be 5 minutes or less. When you're sure that that side won't come loose while you work, repeat the process on the other side. Give your purse about an hour to dry before using it, and enjoy seeing your old favorite shirt anytime you need some change!

PART 3

FOR THE HOME

Need something beautiful to decorate your home? Something to help you get and stay organized? Something comfortable to sink into at the end of a long day? You'll find everything you need for the home in this part!

DIY décor is so satisfying, because it's a way of seeing projects that you're proud of and that were custom-made for your own needs, on a daily basis. Fortunately, the easy-going fabric from T-shirts can be stuffed, stretched, and altered to create a wide range of soft and comfortable items to enjoy in your home. From storage and organization to pretty looks for all the seasons, you can save money and make exactly what you need when you combine retired T-shirts with everyday household items.

If you dabble in sewing or have a friend who does, you know that a pincushion is one of the staple sewing accessories. It's out on the table all the time, so having a pincushion that's also pretty is always a plus! This little Mason Jar Pincushion gives you more than great style. The extra storage in the Mason jar base is a great way to hold extra pins, small spools, or even a little sewing kit. You can scale this design to whatever size jar best suits your needs—if the half-pint jelly jar shown in the pictures isn't enough, Mason jars come in several sizes, giving you plenty of storage options.

Materials

2 oversized circles of T-shirt fabric (cut a diameter twice the size of your jar lid)

Polyester stuffing

Mason jar with ring and lid

Jewelry glue

1 circle cut from card stock or heavy paper, the same size as the Mason jar lid

Optional: Embellishment, like a tiny rolled rosette or button

1 On one of the circles, add a large handful of stuffing on top, in the center. Position the jar lid, topside down, on the stuffing. Run a line of glue along the outer groove of the inside of the jar lid, and carefully gather and glue the edges of the fabric circles to the underside of the lid. When the inner layer is secure, glue the second fabric circle to the inner layer.

2 To cover up the messy underside of the lid, glue your circle of card stock or heavy paper to the inside of the lid.

3 Assemble the jar as you normally would, pushing the pincushion up through the ring of the Mason jar. You can now screw it onto the jar's base, so fill up that jar with your favorite supplies! The fabric around the inside of the ring will prevent the lid from screwing all the way closed, but you will be able to close it halfway. Screwing it on tightly now will help compress the fabric layers, making it easier to close in the future. If you'd like, add a small embellishment to your jar to make it more personal or decorative. Ribbons, buttons, or fabric flowers make great additions, and can be glued directly onto the ring on the front or around the sides with jewelry glue.

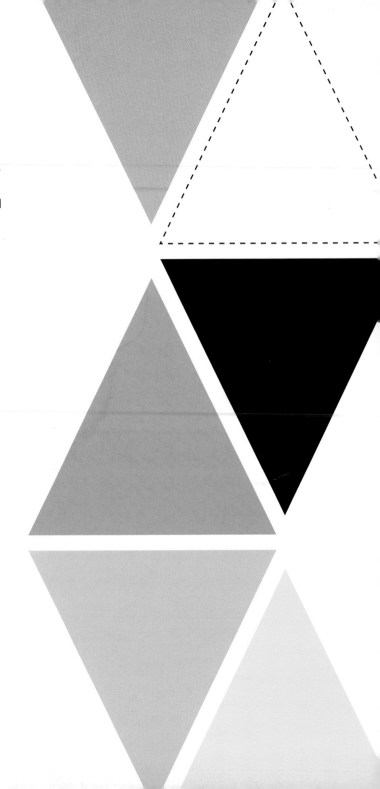

This Loom-Woven Hot Pad may be a basic craft, but it's the project that gave me my start in fiber arts so many years ago, when I made probably a hundred hot pads at summer camp. Weaving is easy, it's satisfying, and it's something anyone can master! All you need is an inexpensive loom, a pair of scissors, and 2 long T-shirt sleeves to make these colorful kitchen accessories. Make some up to match your dishes or your kitchen décor, and serve up more than just a meal with this project.

Materials

1 long-sleeved adult T-shirt (or 2 T-shirts in coordinating colors)
Scissors
Weaving loom

1 Remove each sleeve from the T-shirt (or one sleeve from each T-shirt if you are using two), then cut each sleeve into 18 1"-wide loops. Check the number of pegs on your loom before you begin; typically there are 18 pegs on each side, but if your loom has a different number, cut a number of loops to match.

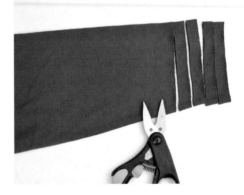

2 Stretch half the loops vertically across the loom, filling all the pegs.

3 Weave the other half of the loops through horizontally. A simple over-under alternating pattern works just fine for this craft.

4 When your hot pad is fully woven, bind it off, beginning at a corner. To do this, take the two end-most loops and pass the second one through the hole of the first one. Then, take the third loop and pass it through the hole in the second loop, and so on. When you get to the corner, continue on as you did for the side.

5 When you reach the final loop, tie it off in a knot. To do this, pass the end of the loop under your beginning loop, and then pass it through the hole you created.

T-SHIRT TIPS!

Create patterns by mixing colors! You can create a checkerboard look by using one color for the vertical loops, and another color for the horizontal loops. Or, create a color-blocked pattern by using 9 loops of one color and 9 loops of another in each direction when you weave.

This practical and pretty project is a testament to how versatile T-shirts really are. Great for holding bathroom essentials, craft room supplies, or almost anything, these unique, braided bowls are great conversation pieces as well. You don't need any special weaving techniques; this fiber bowl is made from one long, coiled braid, held together with the most basic of hand stitches.

Materials

15–20' of T-Shirt Yarn, cut into 3 strands of equal length to make a bowl 4" in diameter and approximately 3" tall (see the "How to Make T-Shirt Yarn" instructions earlier in the book)

Scissors

Needle and approximately 5' of coordinating thread

1 Tie together your 3 strands of T-Shirt Yarn at one end, and cut off the tails next to the knot. Braid the strands tightly. When you get to the end of the fabric, tie an overhand knot to secure the braid. You should have a long braid with a final length of about 5–6'.

2 Trim the loose ends close to the end knot, and begin coiling the braid around the knot to create a flat base. Use the needle and thread to stitch the coils together, placing stitches ¼–½" apart.

3 Continue coiling until your base is approximately 3" in diameter, stitching rows together as you go. Then, add the next row slightly larger, and the following row slightly larger still, so that the shape curves upward to form the sides of your bowl.

5 When your bowl is the height you want, tie an overhand knot in your braid. Secure this end to the row beneath it with thread, cut the excess from the end, and then sew the knot itself to the row beneath. This bowl is very flexible, but it's surprisingly sturdy! You'll love filling it with candy, spare buttons, jewelry, or whatever you like.

4 When stitching the sides together, stitch upward into the bottom of the top row, and downward into the top of the bottom row, alternating every few centimeters. This basic basting stitch goes quite quickly. After connecting 3 or 4 rows, you may find that you have a nicely sized bowl. (You can, of course, continue coiling until you get any dimensions you like.)

Dryer balls are a brilliant laundry aid. They help to reduce the drying time of your clothes by keeping them separated from each other during the drying process. If you're the type who loves home maintenance hacks or just being more energy efficient, this is an experiment you will want to try! You just need a tightly packed ball for great bounce, and a fiber covering to reduce noise. You may have seen some lovely wool-felted options in specialty stores or at craft fairs, but a fabric-covered tennis ball works great too—for a fraction of the cost.

Materials

1 sleeve from a long-sleeved T-shirt with stretchy cuff
1 tennis ball
Needle and 18–24" of coordinating thread

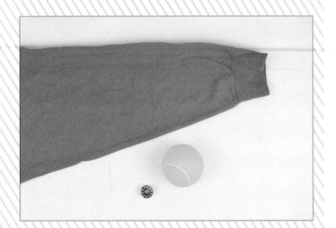

1   Take your T-shirt sleeve and wrap the raw edge around the ball as tightly as possible. Dryer balls work best when the fabric is tightly stretched, so keep the tension throughout this project.

2   At the edge of the ball, twist the sleeve, keeping the fabric tight.

3 Reach inside the sleeve and grab the tennis ball. Pull the sleeve off your arm, turning it inside out, then double it back over the ball.

4 Repeat this step, twisting the fabric at the edge of the ball to keep it tight and then pulling the shirt sleeve back around the ball, until the whole sleeve has been used to cover the ball tightly.

5 When just the cuff remains, thread your needle with double thread and securely stitch the edge of the cuff to the fabric covering the ball. This will ensure that it doesn't unravel when bouncing around, load after load in your dryer. When you've stitched all the way around the ball, knot the two ends of the thread together. Repeat this for as many dryer balls as you wish to make!

T-SHIRT TIPS!

If you don't have a tennis ball handy, raid your fabric scraps! Tightly wound strips of T-shirt fabric have enough bounce to work just as well as a tennis ball. Simply follow these instructions and cover your ball-shaped core in the same way as you would a tennis ball.

SCENTED DRAWER SACHETS

Scented sachets go back for centuries, so this project certainly isn't a new invention. It is, however, a wonderful way to reuse old T-shirts that may have sentimental value while adding a scent that you love to drawers and small spaces—for just pennies apiece! These Scented Drawer Sachets are easy and make up in about 5 minutes each, with no sewing required, which also makes them nice to put together for a last-minute gift. The materials here are what you need to make one sachet, but you can easily multiply to make up whole sets!

Materials

2 (4" × 4") squares of T-shirt fabric
16" of ⅝" iron-on seam adhesive
Iron
⅓–½ cup of uncooked white rice
10–12 drops of your favorite essential oil(s)
Pinking shears or scissors

1 Iron your seam adhesive onto all 4 edges of a fabric square (if the fabric you're using has a design on the front, do this on the back). Then, remove the paper backing, place the other fabric square on top (facing up if the fabric has a design), and iron it closed on 3 of the sides, creating a pouch. Allow it to cool fully, which should only take a minute or two, before continuing.

2 As your adhesive is cooling, add 10–12 drops of your favorite essential oil, or a blend of oils, to your dry rice. Then pour the rice into your sachet.

3 Iron the last side closed, and trim off any uneven edges with pinking shears or scissors. Using pinking shears gives you a pretty zigzag edge, which makes for a professional-looking finish to your sachets!

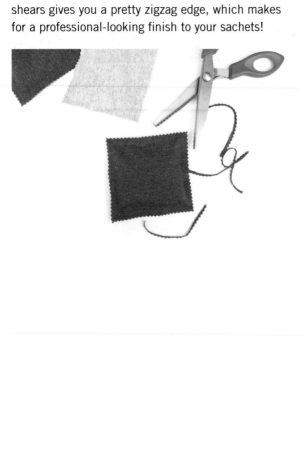

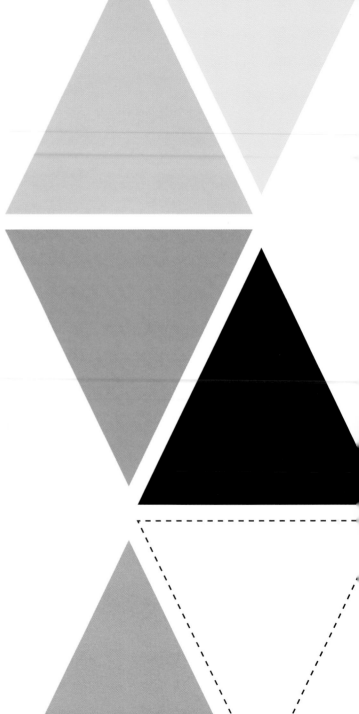

In your home, there are likely spaces that could use a small, brightly colored bin. These sweet Fabric Storage Bins are both simple and sturdy, and they're so easy to make! Make small bins to hold craft supplies like buttons or bobbins, and large bins to organize brushes or tools. You can also use them purely to brighten someone's day, because the simple style and ribbon ties make these great gift baskets! The dimensions are easily adjusted for any length, width, or depth.

Materials

Wax paper to protect your work surface
1 ounce fabric stiffener
1 ounce water
Disposable plastic bowl
1 (8" or 12") square of T-shirt fabric
Pinking shears or scissors
⅛" hole punch
32" of slim ribbon in a coordinating color

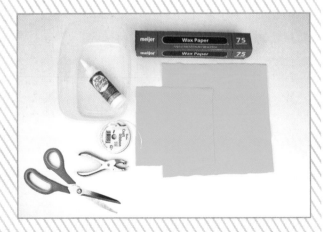

1 First, protect your work surface by laying out wax paper. Then, in a disposable plastic bowl (or one you use just for crafts), mix a 1:1 solution of fabric stiffener and water. Saturate your fabric square, and then squeeze the excess liquid from it.

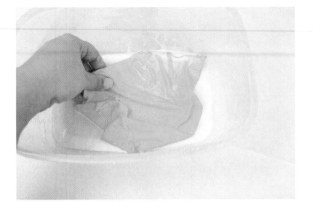

2 Smooth the wet fabric square out onto the wax paper. The edges may roll slightly; if you can't get them to flatten, just focus on the center of the panel. Any wrinkles you leave in this step will become permanent, so take a moment to get the fabric as smooth as possible. Next, allow the fabric to dry fully; this may happen overnight or it may take up to 24 hours.

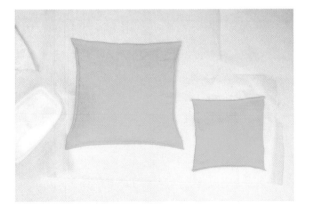

3 Cut away any rough or rolled edges. Pinking shears work well for this step because they give your edges a decorative finish. If your piece is no longer square but more rectangular, that's no problem! As long as all your corners are cut at right angles, both squares and rectangles will make useful bins.

4 Starting at any corner, use your hole punch to punch a small hole ¼" down from the cut edge and 2" from the corner. Each of the 4 corners will need a pair of these punched holes.

5 Pinch a corner, matching up the punched holes. Pass an 8" length of ribbon through the matched holes and tie it in a bow, to create the sides of your bin. For a more rustic or masculine design, you could also just tie a knot, using a shorter length of twine or grosgrain ribbon. Repeat this step for the remaining 3 corners.

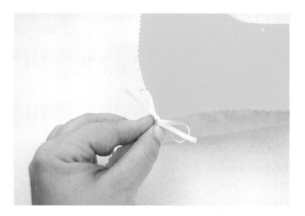

T-SHIRT TIPS!

The distance from the corner at which you punch the holes will determine the height of your bin. Punching the holes 2" from the corner will create a 2"-high side. Experiment with various dimensions! Your bin will be most stable if the height does not exceed the length or width of the base.

you
are
my
sunshine

Looking for an easy way to decorate empty walls? You can create easy artwork by stretching a T-shirt over a blank canvas. Put your favorite old tees on display for a retro theme, or grab a bright shirt and spray bottle of bleach to design something brand new.

Materials

1 T-shirt

Scissors

Freezer paper

Iron

1–2 ounces of liquid chlorine bleach in a spray bottle

Masking tape

1 (12" × 18") stretched canvas

Staple gun

1. Use your scissors to cut a 14" × 20" panel from the body of your T-shirt. This will allow 1" on each side to stretch and staple to your canvas. If you're using any other size of canvas, you can simply lay it out on your T-shirt and cut an extra 1" along each side.

T-SHIRT TIPS!

You can make T-shirt artwork using any size canvas! If you're using a shirt that already has a design, you can match the canvas size to the shirt. When you cut the panel from your shirt, just add 2" to both the length and the width to allow for stretching and stapling it to your frame.

2 Draw or trace a quote or design onto the unwaxed side of the freezer paper, then use your scissors to cut out what you just drew. If you have an electronic or manual cutting machine, you can also die-cut the paper. Note that when using bleach, basic designs and big block letters work best. Lay your design out on the T-shirt fabric (wax side facing down) and when you're happy with how it looks, iron the letters or design onto the shirt panel to create an instant, temporary stencil to aid in your design!

3 Tape your panel to a vertical surface and spray it with bleach. It is best if you can do this step outside, or even in a space that's easy to wipe down, like the inside of your shower. Be very careful not to get the bleach on yourself, your clothing, your upholstery, or any other fibers, or you will bleach them, too. A little goes a long way, so spray from a distance, and wait a minute between sprays to allow the fabric to lighten up. Don't soak the fabric, especially near your paper stencil, because it can easily seep under the edges and blur your design. You should only need 2 or 3 sprays of bleach to cover the whole area. If you want the bleached areas to be lighter, allow the shirt to dry

for at least 30 minutes before giving them a second pass, because bleached areas will continue to lighten as they dry.

4 Allow your shirt to dry, remove it from the panel or wall, then peel off the stencil(s) and remove the masking tape. You may find that it begins to peel on its own as it dries, and that's fine. It's a temporary bond, which makes it easy to remove, and it also leaves no residue behind.

5 Wrap your shirt panel around the canvas, stretching it evenly and tightly. Staple the edge to the frame every few inches.

6 When you get to the corners, fold the shirt just as you would if you were wrapping a gift, and secure the wrap with a couple of staples. The key is keeping tension on the fabric so that it wraps neatly.

If you're short on space for planters in your home or on your patio, elevate them! This easy Knotted Hanging Planter will hold nearly any size pot, and it's a colorful way to add flowers, succulents, or even herbs to small spaces. All you need is 10 minutes, an old tee, and a pair of scissors for an instant and unique hanging planter!

Materials

32' of T-Shirt Yarn (see the "How to Make T-Shirt Yarn" instructions earlier in the book)

Scissors

Potted plant

1 Cut 4 strands of T-Shirt Yarn 8' long. Lay out 3 of them side by side and find their center point. Then, tie the fourth strand around the other 3 at that center point. This will give you 8 equal-length strands, all with a central knot.

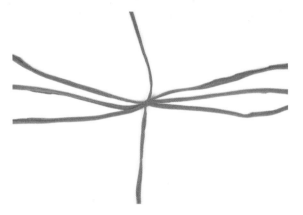

2 About 1" from the center knot, tie 2 adjacent strands together with an overhand knot.

3   Repeat this step for the remaining 6 strands, knotting each pair 1" from the center. You will now have 4 doubled strands coming from the center knot.

4   Separate each pair of strands, and match them with the strand on the other side of the one they're tied to. At 1" from the first round of knots, tie each set of newly paired strands in a knot. You're creating a sort of net to support the pot.

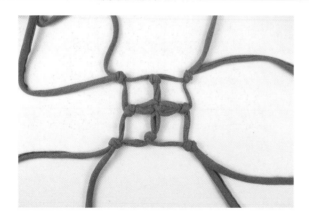

5   Separate the strands again, and pair them with the adjacent strand on the other side. Make a knot 2" from the previous knot, so that the net lays flat. Then, make your next set of knots 4" from the previous knots. At this point, your hanger will support nearly any size planter.

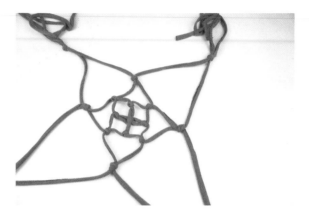

6   Tie a final overhand knot in the end of all the strands, connecting them together. Be sure this knot is tight; double-check by pulling each strand individually to get it as tight as possible. This is the knot that will support the weight of the planter, which isn't a problem because T-Shirt Yarn is great for making tight knots. It's stretchy enough that you can knot it very tightly, and the texture keeps those knots tight. Trim any uneven tails, leaving at least 1" of length. Now, just slip your plant inside, center it, and hang it from a ceiling hook!

INSTANT THROW PILLOW

Do you have a throw pillow that needs an instant update? Maybe you spilled something on it, are looking for a brighter color, or are just plain bored with the old style. Fortunately, a long-sleeved T-shirt can give you a brand-new look in minutes. It only takes a few hand stitches or a well-placed brooch, and no one will ever guess that your new cover had a previous life as a shirt. What's even better is that there's no cutting necessary, so if you opt for a pin to finish off this project, you can even wear the shirt again.

Materials

1 long-sleeved T-shirt
1 throw pillow or pillow form, 16" or smaller
Needle and about 12" of thread, or a decorative pin or brooch

1. Place the pillow inside the shirt near the top. Fold the neck opening down over the pillow, and the bottom hem of the shirt up, to cover the pillow completely.

2. Next, fold in the sides of the shirt, covering the hem and neck folds. Twist the sleeves together, passing them vertically over the top and bottom of the pillow.

3 Flip the pillow over, stretching the arms across the front until they meet.

4 Stitch the sleeves together with a needle and thread, and pull the thread tightly to gather the sleeves together. Add a clip or brooch to cover the seam. For a no-sew option, simply overlap the sleeves and use a decorative brooch to pin them together!

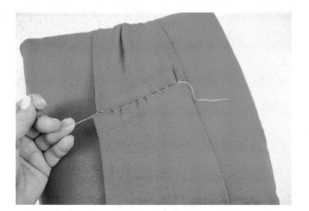

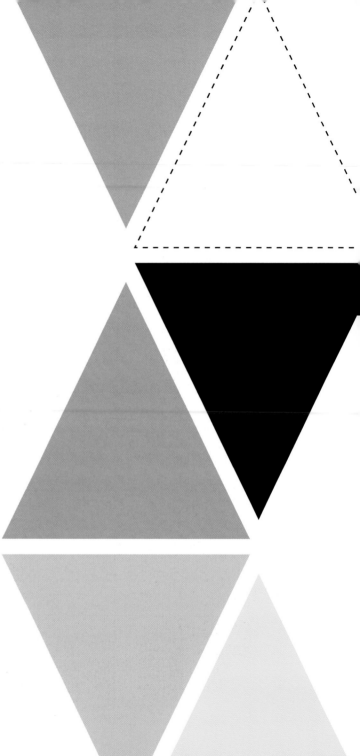

Whether you have kids or pets who love making their home on the floor, or just want to add a fluffy pillow to a couch or bed, this puffy Round Lounge Pillow is perfect—with no sewing required. It's soft and comfortable, just like your favorite old shirt, and what's better than that?

Materials

1 long-sleeved T-shirt
Scissors
2 scraps of T-shirt fabric, any color
5–6' of ⅝" iron-on seam adhesive
Iron
12 ounces polyester stuffing
Optional: Button or brooch

1 Cut 2 circles, as large as you can cut, from the body of your T-shirt. Starting with one circle, find the center and then pinch the fabric to gather it (if your fabric has two sides, do this on what will be the inside of the pillow). Tie one of your fabric scraps tightly around the pinched center. Repeat the process on the second circle. This will create pleats, to add a little extra texture and pouf to the pillow.

2 Iron your seam adhesive all the way around the edge of the outside of one of your circles (not the side with the tie). This may look like the wrong side, but this edge will be tucked into the interior of the pillow at the end. Using several strips, 6–8" long, is typically easier to manage when you're trying to iron in a circle. Note that if you have basic sewing skills, this works up even faster by using the sewing machine. You can certainly sew instead of using the adhesive!

4 Reach inside the hole you created and grab the other side of the pillow. Pull it out through the hole, turning it right-side out. Iron all along the edge, to smooth the seam.

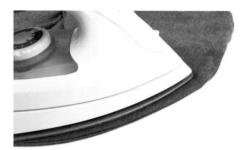

3 Remove the paper backing, line up the edges of your fabric, and iron again. Then iron the 2 circles together so that the outer sides face each other. Leave a 4–6" gap open. You'll need the hole for the next step. Allow the adhesive to cool completely.

5 Stuff it! You decide how soft or firm you want it to be. When it comes to stuffing, adding a little more than you think you need is always a good idea.

6   Iron the final gap shut. You may find it helpful to pin it closed while you iron, or immediately afterward, while you allow the adhesive to cool. While hot, the seam will easily pull apart, especially if you've added lots of stuffing.

7   If desired, add a simple brooch or a button for instant embellishment! Just fasten it on in the center of the pillow.

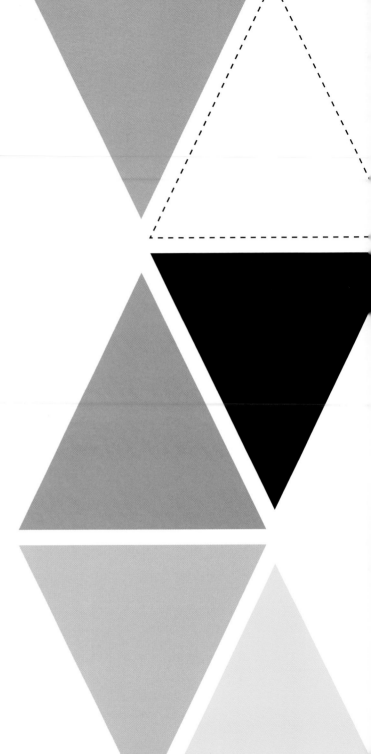

POMPOM GARLAND

When you want to whip up a little festive decoration for a party, for a holiday, or simply just because, easy garland is a great way to go. If you have a few yards left on your skeins of T-Shirt Yarn, you can turn them into little pompoms and string them up for instant fun! A pompom maker is inexpensive and helps you get a great, full shape, and you can easily make up a dozen poms or more in just an hour!

Materials

12 strips of 1" T-Shirt Yarn, 8–10' long each in various colors (see the "How to Make T-Shirt Yarn" instructions earlier in the book)

Pompom maker

Scissors

8" of coordinating embroidery floss for each pompom

1 (6') length of T-Shirt Yarn in a coordinating color from which to hang your finished pompoms

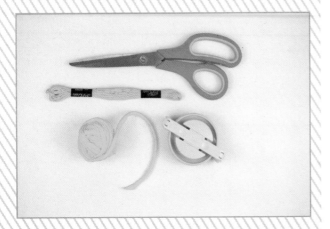

1. Begin by wrapping 8–10' of yarn around the pompom maker. Note that each brand of pompom maker works slightly differently, so check the instructions included with yours.

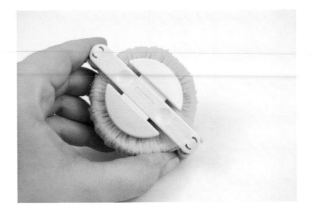

2. When you have wrapped the yarn, use sharp scissors to cut down the center, creating all of the uniformly sized pompom strings.

3 Use the coordinating embroidery floss to tie the pompom around the center tightly, and then remove it from the pompom maker.

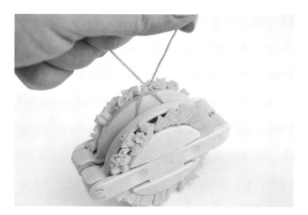

4 Shake the pompom and it will puff up to that nice round pompom shape. Leave the tails of the embroidery floss long. Repeat all previous steps until you have 12 pompoms.

5 Using the long embroidery floss tails, tie the finished pompoms to your length of T-Shirt Yarn, spacing them about 6" apart. Trim the excess floss. You can of course make your garland in whatever length you need, and adjust the spacing as necessary!

NO-SEW STUFFED
PUMPKIN DECORATION

This festive fall decoration is easy to make, and trying colors other than classic orange is a great way to enhance your current décor. There's no sewing or glue necessary, just fabric and stuffing! You can make up a little patch of pumpkins to set out on a table, a mantel, or any place that can use a touch of rustic autumn charm.

Materials

1 square of T-shirt fabric, any size from 8–24"

1–2 ounces polyester stuffing, depending on the size of your fabric squares

1 rubber band

2' of T-Shirt Yarn (see the "How to Make T-Shirt Yarn" instructions earlier in the book)

Scissors

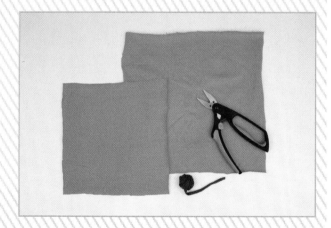

1 Place a large ball of stuffing in the center of your fabric square. You want enough stuffing so that the sides of the square just overlap when you gather them together.

2 Gather the fabric up around the stuffing, pulling the sides of the square first and the corners last. Wrap a rubber band around the excess fabric to hold it steady while you work. Tightly tie the T-Shirt Yarn around the base of your stem just below the rubber band, leaving a tail a few inches long.

3   Use the tail to wrap the long end up the "stem" for about 2". When you reach that point, wrap back downward, over the first layer of yarn. When you reach the base, tie the two ends together in a double knot or square knot. Trim any excess yarn you may have, so that your tails are no longer than 2–3".

4   Cut the excess fabric off at the top of the stem. There will be many layers, so you may have to trim just a little bit at a time. Make as many pumpkins as you like to fill your space!

Taking down your winter décor tends to make your home look a little bit empty! So, when you take down the wreaths and hangings, it's nice to have a bright springtime piece to put up in their place. This fabric-wrapped Spring Flower Wreath has a bouquet of rolled roses to welcome spring with a pop of color!

Materials

1 T-shirt

Scissors

1 (16") round wreath form

5 or 6 sewing pins

Fabric glue

Enough T-shirts or T-shirt scraps to cut 12–18 strips of 1"-wide T-Shirt Yarn in coordinating colors (for rosette embellishments), in varying lengths from 6–18" (see the "How to Make T-Shirt Yarn" instructions earlier in the book)

Sawtooth hanger

1　Remove the center panel of the shirt between the arms and the bottom hem. Fold it in half vertically, and make your cuts 4" apart. Cut this fabric in the same way you would cut your T-Shirt Yarn. Open the panel, and complete your cuts using the method outlined in the "How to Make T-Shirt Yarn" section at the beginning of the book. Overall, you will need 10–12' of 4"-wide T-shirt fabric for this project.

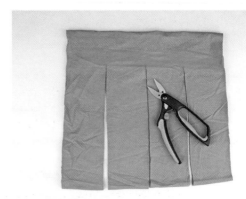

2　Wrap your 4"-wide fabric tightly around the wreath form, covering it completely. You may find it helpful to use a pin when you get started wrapping, and the foam is soft and thick enough that pins are safe to use in this project. When your form is completely covered, glue or pin the end on the back to finish your wreath form.

3 Now, make 12–18 rolled rosettes to add to the wreath. Using 3 or 4 different colors in varying sizes will give you a good visual variety. To make your rosettes, tie a knot at the end of a 1"-wide fabric strip. This will be the center of your rosette. Small rosettes will only require about 6" of fabric, and larger rosettes may take up to 18", depending on the size you prefer.

4 Gently twist the fabric strip, and wind it around the center knot. Add dots of fabric glue as you go, to help secure it.

5 When your rosette is the size you want (varying sizes between 1" and 3" work really well together for this design), just fold the tail end of the fabric strip over the back of the rosette, and use fabric glue to glue it down. This will secure the petals of your rosette. Alternately, you could cut a small circle the size of your rosette and glue that to the back, but because you're making roses in so many different sizes, and because they won't be worn or subjected to anything high-impact, a simple glued fold is sufficient to keep it together. Once the rosette is secure, trim away the excess fabric.

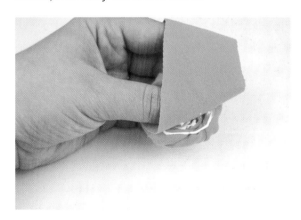

6 When you have between 12 and 18 rosettes, glue them on to your wrapped wreath with fabric glue to create a small corner bouquet. If you want to keep going, though, make as many flowers as you want!

7 Finally, you can easily add a hanger to the back of your wreath by pinning a sawtooth hanger at the top with 2 sewing pins. The foam and fabric are quite lightweight, so the pins are sufficient to hold the hanger in place.

PART 4

GREAT GIFTS

The most rewarding thing about DIY is giving heartfelt and handmade gifts to the people you care about. If you love making gifts, love wrapping them, and love adding your personal touch, the projects in this part are perfect for you! Here, you'll find projects that range from practical to pampering, like the Coffee Cozy, Aromatherapy Neck Pillow, and Rolled Rosette Key Chain, along with items that put beautiful finishing touches on a gift, like the Floral Gift Ribbons and the Stamped and Embellished Gift Tags. And, if you want to keep the number on the price tag down, you're going to be even more pleased. As you probably know, there are ways to give thoughtful gifts no matter your budget, but recycled gifts can be tricky! Fortunately, despite the shoestring budget they require, these simple projects let you show how much you care, without gifting something that looks like an old T-shirt. Happy gifting!

Adding a simple ruffled rose and T-Shirt Yarn to a present is a great alternative to expensive cords and ribbons—and your recipient can reuse and enjoy it after opening her gift, too! If your friends or loved ones are avid recyclers, they'll really appreciate you giving beautiful new life to a shirt once destined for the donation pile.

Materials

Needle and 12–18" of coordinating thread
1 strip of 1"-wide T-Shirt Yarn, 24" long
Fabric glue
2 (2"-diameter) fabric circles in the same color as your T-Shirt Yarn
Enough T-Shirt Yarn to tie around your package (see the "How to Make T-Shirt Yarn" instructions earlier in the book)

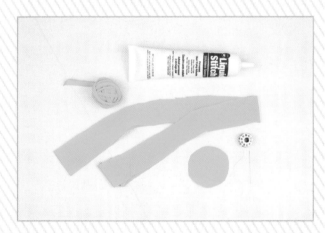

1 Thread your needle, and tie a knot at the bottom of your fabric strip in the center with your thread, securing one end directly to the fabric. Using a simple basting stitch (an over-under stitch), stitch vertically along the center of your fabric strip using ¼" stitches. It's not essential to keep these stitches uniform, so don't worry if they're a little messy—just try to keep them as close to the center of the strip as possible.

2 When you get to the end of the fabric strip, pull the thread tight and gather the fabric into small ruffles until your fabric strip has been reduced to about half its original length. (For example, if you started with an 18" strip, make the final length a ruffled piece 9" long.) Tie off the thread securely at the end of the gathered fabric strip, then fold the ruffled strip in half along the line of stitching and roll the fabric into a spiral along the stitched edge, to create one flat side and one ruffled side.

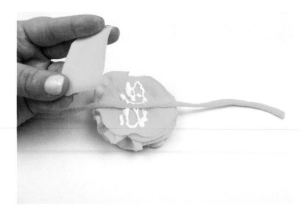

3 Cover the flat side of your ruffled rose with fabric glue, and secure it with a fabric circle.

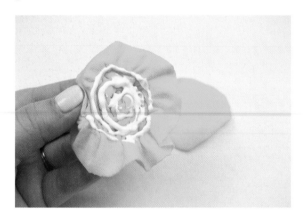

4 Cut a length of T-Shirt Yarn about 4" long, and lay it across the back of the flower, centering it. Add a second layer of glue, and glue on the second fabric circle, securing the yarn between the 2 layers. This will give you a way to tie the rose onto your package later. Allow the flower to dry overnight.

5 Wrap your package in colorful paper or tissue, or really get into the recycling spirit by using newspaper or a paper grocery bag! Tie your package up with the rest of the T-Shirt Yarn, and attach the ruffled rose to the knot for a beautifully floral-themed look.

T-SHIRT TIPS!

Instead of just tying the rose onto the package, take it one step further! In place of string, add a hair clip or brooch base to secure the rose to the knot, to make an instant accessory for your recipient that's easy to use over and over again.

HOMEMADE
BREAD WRAPS

If you do a lot of baking, then you probably give a lot of baked goods as gifts. After all, everyone loves homemade treats! But while there are lots of pretty containers for items like cookies, breads are often just wrapped in foil or plastic wrap. This T-shirt project makes your homemade breads look just as special as the care that went into baking them, and it keeps them fresh, too!

Materials

1 (12" × 16") panel of T-shirt fabric for a mini-loaf (or the appropriate size for your loaf pan)

1 piece of freezer paper, measured to match your T-shirt fabric

Iron

Scissors or pinking shears

Fabric or paper tape, like washi tape or masking tape

Baker's twine, ribbon, or cord, and an optional tag

1. Place the freezer paper on the inside of your T-shirt fabric, waxy-side down and paper-side up. On medium-high heat without steam, iron the paper to the fabric. Within a few seconds, the wax layer will melt enough to grip the fabric. It will not be a permanent bond, so handle it gently, but it will stick to the fabric enough to trim and wrap the bread. Use your scissors to trim away any uneven edges, and you will be left with a panel that is fabric on one side and paper on the other, with a layer of wax in between that will keep your bread fresh.

2. Next, wrap your bread, just as you would a present, keeping the seam at the bottom of the loaf.

3 Secure the seams with paper tape or fabric tape. Washi tape comes in lots of pretty designs, but regular masking tape will also work well to hold the seams closed. (Scotch tape just isn't sticky enough to grip fabric seams.)

4 Tie some twine or ribbon securely over the bread to help hold the seams closed, and you can also add a small tag to identify what's inside. Your bread will stay fresh for days thanks to the freezer paper, and the gift presentation will make your recipient feel special!

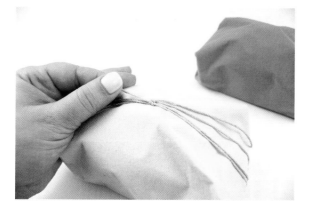

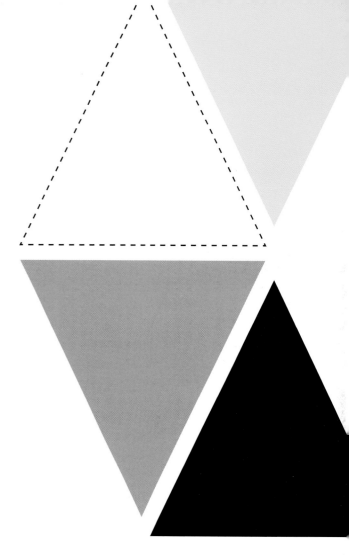

STAMPED AND
EMBELLISHED GIFT TAGS

Every special gift deserves a special tag, and these Stamped and Embellished Gift Tags deliver! Using fabric stiffener on T-shirt fabric gives it the feel of card stock or chipboard, but it won't rip or tear. You can embellish it like you would any other type of tag, with stamps, buttons, ribbons, markers, and more. Pair a stamped tag with Floral Gift Ribbons (project in this chapter), and your recipient will be so surprised at what you've made just by recycling T-shirts.

Materials

Wax paper to protect your work surface

¼ ounce of fabric stiffener for each tag you're making

¼ ounce of water for each tag you're making

Disposable plastic bowl

Various scraps of T-shirt fabric at least 1" × 2"

Scissors or pinking shears

Ink pad and stamps, markers, buttons, or other embellishments

⅛" hole punch

6" of twine for each tag you're making

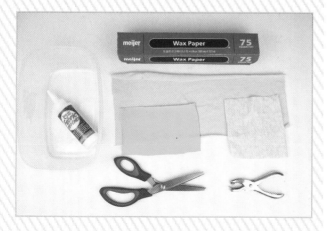

1. First, protect your work surface by laying out wax paper. Then in a disposable plastic bowl (or one you just use for crafts), mix a 1:1 solution of fabric stiffener and water. The amount of solution you need will depend on the number of tags you're making, but for every 4 tags (1" × 2" sized), you'll need about 1 ounce of this mixed solution. Saturate your fabric scrap(s), and squeeze out the excess liquid. If you're making many tags from one fabric scrap, it's not necessary to cut it apart before adding fabric stiffener! In fact, it will cut more easily if you wait until later to cut your tags apart.

2. Smooth out the wet fabric scraps on the wax paper. Any wrinkles you leave in this step will become permanent, so take a moment to get the fabric as smooth as possible. Set the scraps aside and allow them to dry fully. This may happen overnight or it may take up to 24 hours.

3   When your fabric is dry, cut the tags to 1" wide ×
    2" tall, or if they are already that size, trim away
    any rough edges. Trim the top corners off at a
    45-degree angle for a traditionally shaped tag.
    Using pinking shears here gives a more decorative
    look. You can of course cut the tags to any size that
    you desire.

4   Now, get ready to shape and embellish! Collect
    stamps and ink, buttons, stencils, markers, or
    make small fabric flowers to add to the tags. The
    designs you can make are only limited by your
    creativity.

5   Using your hole punch, punch a hole in the top of
    each tag.

6   *For stamped designs:* Experiment with large and
    small stamps. You can use regular scrapbooking ink
    on the stiffened fabric.

7 *For three-dimensional embellishments:* Make small flowers (you can find specific instructions for several styles of fabric flowers in many of the other projects in this book. Check out the Rolled Rosette Hair Pins and Coffee Cozy projects, for instance. Then, attach them to your tags with fabric glue.

8 Finally, tie a 6" piece of twine through the hole of each tag. You can then use the twine to attach a tag to your next gift.

This easy Wine Bag makes up in just minutes, so it's a perfect last-minute solution for wrapping a wine gift. For a more personal touch, you can also stamp or paint it with fabric paint before adding the wine to the bag—it's a great way to help an average (or not so average) bottle of wine to stand out as a special gift, even before it's opened.

Materials

1 sleeve from a long-sleeved T-shirt—women's shirts work best for this project

Scissors

12" of twine or cord

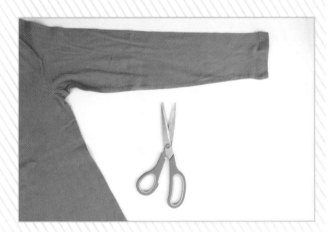

1. To determine how much sleeve you'll need to use, add 3" to the length of the bottle. This can be an informal measurement—you can just slip the bottle into the sleeve to determine the overall length you need.

2. Cut off the sleeve, plus an additional scrap of fabric about 1" wide and a few inches long. Turn the sleeve inside out, and gather the raw end together. Tie it off tightly with the fabric scrap. Trim the excess fabric off as close to the edge as you can. Finally, turn the sleeve right-side out, add the bottle of wine, and then tie it off at the neck with your twine or cord.

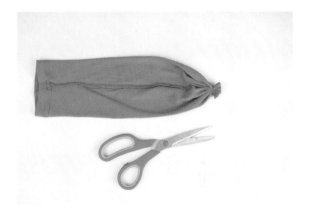

T-SHIRT TIPS!

Does your wine bottle have a flat bottom? If so, it only takes a few more minutes to hand-sew a flat seam, or to use iron-on seam adhesive for the bottom of your wine bag. The knotted style is a perfect quick project—but only for bottles with a concave bottom.

Adding a special touch to your favorite mug is a great way to brighten your morning, and there's just something irresistible about this Coffee Cozy. The exact dimensions of this project will vary depending on the size of your mug or cup, but sizing your own cozy is easy, and it's a great way to make something truly one-of-a-kind.

Materials

1 mug

Measuring tape

2 pieces of T-shirt fabric to fit your mug (see the instructions for details how to get the exact dimensions)

Scissors

8–10" of ⅝"iron-on seam adhesive

Iron

Snaps and snap setter

Needle and 24–36" of coordinating embroidery floss

Optional: Yo-yo maker, button, and fabric glue

1 First, determine the dimensions you need for your cup cozy. Measure around your mug, inside the handle, with a measuring tape. Add 1" to this length. Next, measure the height of the handle at its widest point. This latte-style mug measured 12" around with a 2" handle, so this fabric was cut to 13" × 2".

2 Cut 4 pieces of iron-on seam adhesive to span the width of your fabric, and then place 2 pieces side by side across both ends of one layer. Then, remove the paper backing, place your second fabric layer on top of the first, and iron your two pieces of fabric together to create a double layer. This will stiffen and support the ends, which is important in the next steps.

3 Use your snap setter to add a snap to each end of the fabric strip you have cut, ¾" from the end. Each brand and style of snap setter will work a little differently, so refer to the directions for your model. No matter the style, though, you will be crimping together a base and prongs through two layers of fabric for each side of the snap. Don't let snaps intimidate you—they're actually quite easy! But if you feel that snaps are out of your league, you can also opt for stitch-on Velcro to create your closure.

4 Use your scissors to gently shape the ends of the cozy so that they look smooth, then narrow them to the width of the handle where it attaches to the mug. Cutting a gentle curve on each side will make your cozy look more professionally finished, and it's a step made easy by the iron-on adhesive between the layers. It can also help your cozy to fit better inside the mug handle. Next, add a basting stitch of embroidery floss along each long side of the cozy. This will serve to hold the layers together, and the simple over-under stitch makes your edges more decorative. Tie a knot on the underside of the cozy to finish off the stitching.

5 Your coffee cozy is perfectly functional as it is, but you may want to go one step further and add a bit of embellishment. A little fabric yo-yo makes a fun, floral addition to your design. With a yo-yo maker, you can make one in just a couple of minutes! Insert your fabric between the two sides of the yo-yo maker, and trim off any excess.

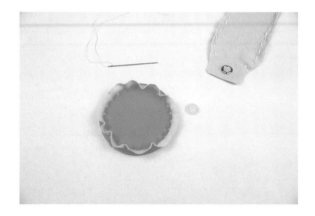

6 Follow the stitching lines on the back of the yo-yo maker. Pop your work out of the maker once you've gone all the way around.

8 Find a spot to glue your floral embellishment on with fabric glue, and give it about an hour to dry. Then, snap your cozy onto your favorite mug and enjoy!

7 Cinch the thread together to create the yo-yo, and tie the two threads together. This is a great time to add a button center, to turn your yo-yo into a rustic-looking flower.

BRAIDED SPIRAL COASTERS

This great home project will help you protect your tables from water rings and recycle your old tees at the same time! These easy Braided Spiral Coasters require just basic braiding and a bit of glue and cork. They're a great way to use up those last few feet of T-Shirt Yarn you have left over, or if you prefer, just use just one skein to create a monochromatic set.

Materials

12 strips of 1" T-Shirt Yarn, 4' long each, in various colors (see the "How to Make T-Shirt Yarn" instructions earlier in the book)

Scissors

Fabric glue

A roll of craft cork or 4 (3½") round cork coaster bases

1 For your first coaster, choose 3 strips of yarn. Tie an overhand knot at the end of the three pieces, and braid it into one long braid. Tie off the braid at the end with a second overhand knot.

2 Trim the excess tails off one end knot and begin coiling it, adding dots of fabric glue every few centimeters. It's easiest and most sturdy if you coil it so that the braid lays flat against the inner layers. You'll only see the edge of the braid from the top.

3 When you get to the end, cut the knot off the braid, and add a liberal amount of fabric glue to the loose ends. Glue them firmly to the last coil.

4 Cut 4 circles of 3½" each from your craft cork, or use precut circles to finish the coasters. Add fabric glue to one side of the braided fabric and glue the cork to it, forming the bottom of the coaster. Repeat until you have a whole set of coasters!

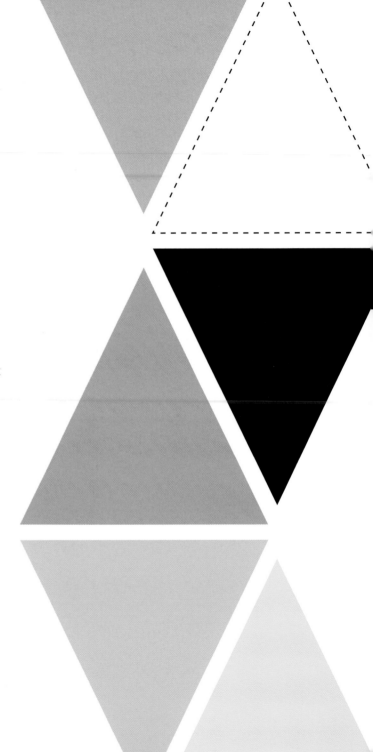

Gifts in jars are so popular right now, and it's no wonder! They're cute, they're useful, and they're a great way to give a handmade gift. Making up a drink mix or a batch of soaking salts lets someone know she is special—without costing you a lot. By recycling a T-shirt to make this pretty ruffled rose jar topper and adding a simple bath soak recipe, you can have a nice gift for less than two dollars each.

Materials

Needle and 12–18" of coordinating thread
1 strip of 1½"-wide T-shirt fabric, 24"
Fabric glue
1 fabric circle 2½" in diameter
Heavy paper or card stock, cut to the same size as your jar lid
1 fabric circle cut to the same size as your jar lid
Half-pint Mason jar with ring and lid
Jewelry glue

1 Thread your needle with 12–18" of thread, and tie a knot at the bottom of your fabric strip in the center with your thread, securing one end directly to the fabric. Using a simple basting stitch (an over-under stitch), stitch vertically using ¼" stitches along the center of your fabric strip. It's not essential to keep these stitches uniform, so don't worry if they're a little messy—just try to keep them as close to the center of the strip as possible.

2 When you get to the end of the fabric strip, pull the thread tight and gather the fabric into small ruffles until your fabric strip has been reduced to about 15" long. Tie off the thread securely at the end of the gathered fabric strip.

3 Fold the ruffled strip in half along the line of stitching.

4 Roll the fabric into a spiral along the stitched edge. This will create one flat side and one ruffled side. Cover the flat side of your ruffled rose with fabric glue, and secure it with the 2½" fabric circle.

5 Glue together the card stock or paper circle and the fabric circle that matches your jar lid size, using a very thin layer of fabric glue. Then, run a line of jewelry glue along the inside of the Mason jar ring.

6 Next, position the circle fabric-side up, and place it into the top of the jar ring so that the ring has a fabric topper that will cover the jar's metal lid. Then, glue the rose to the fabric topper inside the ring.

7 Fill your jar with your gift mix, and cover it tightly!

T-SHIRT TIPS!

If you want to make your own bath salts, just add 5 drops of your favorite essential oil to 1 cup of coarse sea salt. Stir it very well, then add 1 tablespoon of baking soda. Stir again, and store it tightly covered in a half-pint Mason jar. This bath salt soak will last up to a year on the shelf.

Show off your love of recycling with this sweet Rolled Rosette Key Chain! It makes a great gift for new roommates, first-time homeowners, or friends driving a new car, and it's so easy to make. You can even engrave or stamp a message on the back of the key chain, so they're reminded often that you wish them well.

Materials

1 strip of 1"-wide T-shirt fabric or T-Shirt Yarn, 12–14" long
Fabric glue
1 fabric circle, cut to the size of your metal blank
1 (1"-round) metal blank with a hole
1 (12-millimeter) heavy gauge jump ring
1 split key ring
Flat-nosed jewelry pliers
Jewelry glue
Optional: Engraving pen or metal stamps

1 Tie a knot at the end of your strip of yarn to create the center of your rosette.

2 Gently twist the fabric strip, and wind it around the center knot. Add dots of fabric glue as you go to help secure it.

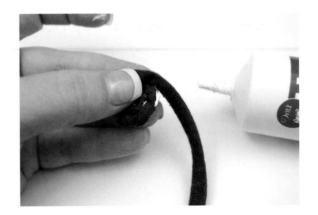

3 When your rosette is slightly over 1" in diameter (or the size that matches your blank), glue the fabric circle to the back of your rosette, taking care to tuck in the loose end.

4 Prepare your metal blank by using the pliers to add the jump ring and split key ring, and if you're going to add a message, engrave or stamp it now!

5 Glue the rosette securely to the metal blank with the jewelry glue. Allow it to dry for at least an hour, and then just add your keys and go!

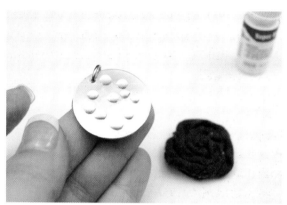

AROMATHERAPY
NECK PILLOW

Pampering and relaxation should be an easy thing, so you shouldn't have to go to a lot of trouble to make something that will help you relax. Fortunately, this project is an easy way to enjoy a bit of aromatherapy and heat therapy. Pamper a friend—or yourself—with this scented pillow that can be microwaved to relax tired muscles. This Aromatherapy Neck Pillow just needs 30 seconds in the microwave to serve as a scented heating pad that can be used to ease mild headaches and shoulder tension.

Materials

1 sleeve from a long-sleeved T-shirt

12" of T-Shirt Yarn, cut into 2 6" pieces (see the "How to Make T-Shirt Yarn" instructions earlier in the book)

Scissors

3–4 cups uncooked (not instant) white rice

30–40 drops of your favorite essential oil(s)

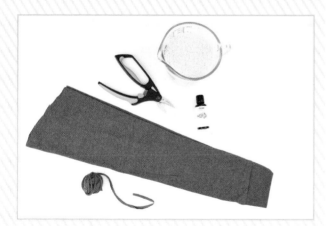

1 Gather the sleeve just above the shirt cuff, and tie it tightly with a 6" piece of T-shirt yarn.

2 Cut off the cuff of the shirt close to the knot. For a more feminine touch, add a dot of glue and tie your yarn in a small bow.

3 Add 8–10 drops of oil for each cup of rice, and stir it well. Let the rice rest for a few minutes to absorb the oils, then pour into the sleeve. Don't overfill it; it only needs to be filled about halfway. Tie off the other end of the sleeve to match the first with the remaining piece of yarn, and enjoy a bit of warm aromatherapy!

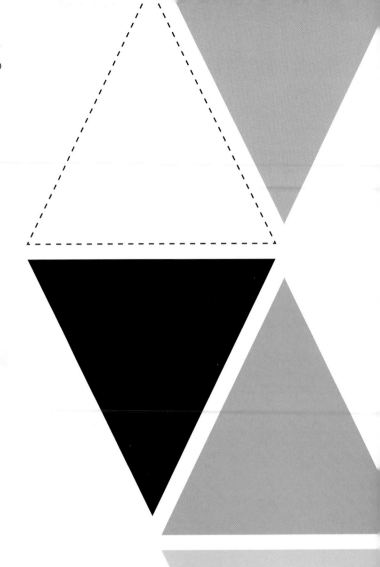

If you're a traveler, you know the simple necessity of catching what sleep you can, when you can. Sometimes that means using a little something extra to block out the light, and this easy Sleep Mask fits the bill! Use a sassy old concert tee or a former favorite comfy tee to express yourself as you relax and rest, or give the gift of a good night's sleep to someone you care about!

Materials

Scrap paper

Marker

Measuring tape

Scissors

3 fabric rectangles, 7½" × 3" each

3–4' of ⅝" iron-on seam adhesive

Iron

16" of elastic cord

Needle and 2–3' of coordinating thread

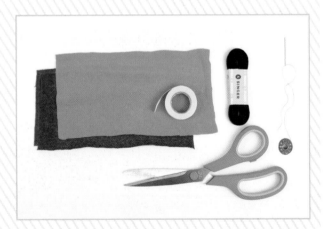

1   Using the scrap paper, marker, measuring tape, and scissors, trace and cut your sleep mask template. You will want to make it 7" wide, and you can adjust the height and nose dimensions to whatever best fits your face. When you're happy with your paper template, trace it onto your fabric, and cut 3 mask layers.

2   Determine which will be your inner, outer, and middle layers. Consider choosing the softest fabric for the inner layers that will be worn against your face, or your favorite color on the outside to show off your style. Then, on medium-high heat with no steam, iron the seam adhesive all the way around the outer edge of your inner layer. This will be the layer that rests against your face.

3 Remove the paper backing from the seam adhesive. Place your middle layer on top of the inner layer, then take your elastic and place it between these layers on one side of the mask, overlapping it about 1" in from the outside edge. Iron the middle and inner layers together and allow your adhesive to cool fully, about 1–2 minutes, before continuing.

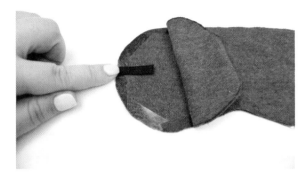

4 Stitch 2 X-shaped stitches through the elastic and both mask layers, one at the end of the elastic, and one close to the edge of the mask. Tie off your thread on the inner layer; because the inner layer is about to be sandwiched between the other layers, it won't matter if the stitching isn't pretty. Repeat the process of ironing and stitching on the other side of the mask.

5 Iron the seam adhesive around the edge of your outer mask layer. If you'd like to add a small cut-out, to make the mask less plain, add a bit of seam adhesive to a corner of the mask, and cut out a small design, like a heart. The remaining adhesive should be slightly larger than the shape you cut. Peel off the paper backing, and iron the outer layer onto the middle layer. Allow a minute or two for your seam adhesive to cool, get some rest, and enjoy your new Sleep Mask!

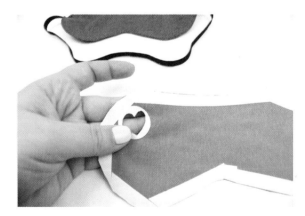

BABY POMPOM HAT

Accessories are for everyone, even the smallest in the family! If you have an upcoming baby shower to attend, make an instant baby hat by recycling the sleeve of an old long-sleeved tee—it's a project you can do in about 10 minutes! The size of the hat will be determined by the style and size shirt you're using, so try to choose stretchy women's shirts for infants. Larger men's shirts make great toddler-sized hats.

Materials

1 sleeve from a long-sleeved T-shirt
Scissors

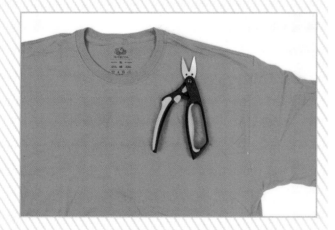

1 Take your shirt sleeve and remove the cuff or hem. Then, cut a 1" strip of fabric, and trim the rest of the sleeve to 16" for babies, or 18" for toddlers.

2 Tuck the smaller end of the sleeve through the larger end, and pull it through so that the smaller half is nested inside the larger half. Line up the raw edges.

3 Cut several 1" strips along the raw edge, leaving 6"
   uncut for an infant-sized hat, and 6½" uncut for a
   toddler-sized one.

5 Pull each strip of fabric so that it rolls slightly, for a
   more finished-looking fringe.

4 Gather the fringe you just cut, and using the strip
   you cut in Step 1, tie the hat tightly at the point
   where the fringe begins.

INDEX

ABOUT THE AUTHOR

Adrianne Surian is a west Michigan wife and mother of two, and an artist, designer, and blogger at *www.happyhourprojects.com*. She has been designing jewelry since friendship bracelets ruled the playground, and crafting since long before it was cool.